BAGS

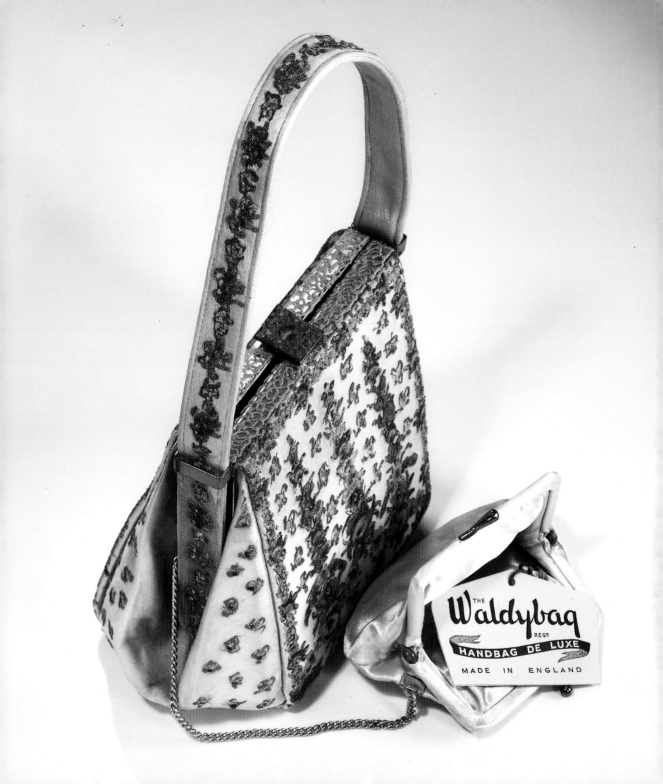

The Waldybag

REG^d

HANDBAG DE LUXE

MADE IN ENGLAND

BAGS

Claire Wilcox

Colour photography by Sara Hodges

V&A Publications

First published by V&A Publications, 1999

Reprinted 2000

V&A Publications
160 Brompton Road
London SW3 1HW

© The Board of Trustees of the
Victoria and Albert Museum 1999

Designed by Broadbase
Photography by Sara Hodges;
V&A Photographic Studio

ISBN 1851772863

A catalogue record for this book is
available from the British Library

Manufactured in China by Imago
Publishing Limited.

Jacket front: Grey flannel
handbag with chrome frame,
bound in black leather and
with lizard handles. British,
c.1932. By Hellstern. The
bag is lined in black moiré,
and is fitted with a mirror
and lipstick pocket and a
loose purse. It is part of an
ensemble that includes
matching belt and shoes.
T.302–1971

Jacket back: Group of
pastel-coloured dupion silk
'Paulton' handbags with
diamanté clasps. British,
1996. By Anya Hindmarch.
Although they recall the
styles and colours of the
1950s, they suit the vogue
for special occasion and
classic bags of the 1990s.
T.470–1996; T.471–1996;
T.472–1996

Frontispiece: Cream satin
evening bag with painted
and glass-bead decoration
and captive purse. British,
early 1950s. By H. Wald &
Co. The unusual decorative
technique was developed
by H. Wald & Co after the
Second World War. Minuscule
glass beads were applied to
the flowers while the paint
was still wet, creating a
glistening, textured effect.
These handbags were
popular with the British
Royal family. The company's
bags were known as
'Waldybags'. T.536–1996

Contents

Acknowledgements

I would like to thank the following colleagues at the V&A for their assistance during the writing of this book: Valerie Mendes, Linda Parry, Susan North, Linda Woolley, Jennifer Wearden, Clare Brown, Julian Bell, Paul Harrison, Ngozi Ikoku, Lucy Pratt, Helen Wilkinson and Debbie Sinfield of the Textiles and Dress Department; and Shaun Cole and Charlotte Cotton of the Prints, Drawings and Paintings Department. I am very grateful to Sara Hodges for her excellent colour photography, and I also thank the staff in the V&A Picture Library.

I would very much like to thank the team at V&A Publications, especially Mary Butler, Miranda Harrison and Valerie Chandler, as well as my editor, Helen Armitage. I would also particularly like to acknowledge the support of the following: Jean and Syd Wilcox, Julian Stair, Rose and Hattie. Finally, I am very grateful to all the designers, donors and other individuals who have made this publication possible.

Opposite Photo from the early 1970s. Regent Street, London. Dressed in white hot pants and knee-high boots, grasping a neat shoulder bag by its straps, a woman strides down the street – in complete contrast to the half-seen figure on the left, with her sensible mac and her plain capacious handbag.

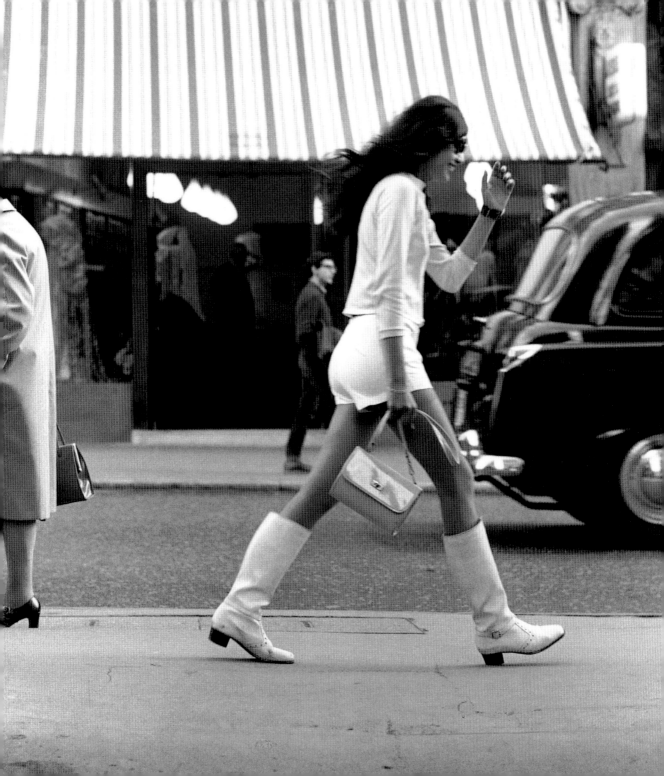

Introduction

The history of the handbag and its small conspirator and close ally, the coin purse, touches upon many different aspects of dress and textiles. Purses and bags have been essential to daily life for as long as people have had money or precious items to be carried. Although often discussed together, the purse has a specific evolution determined by the development of coinage, bills and paper notes and eventually banking. Decoration and embellishment was natural, and purses were the recipient of devoted domestic and professional attention up until the age of mass production. Reflecting changing tastes in needlework and textiles, they have in the past been acquired by museums as examples of diverse needlework techniques rather than fashionable accessories, but, like tiny time capsules, they provide valuable insights into past tastes in dress when much of it has disappeared.

The development of the larger hand-held bag is also determined by function, as a portable container for all the ephemera of private and public life that needed to be carried both inside the house and out, particularly before pockets were developed in the eighteenth century. Its history is also related to needlework, once so important to women's lives. Until the late eighteenth century needlework tools were carried on the person, hanging at the waist or in the pocket, or in work-bags. This was as much for practical reasons as for security, for it was not until the 1700s that the separate work box developed, freeing the work-bag to evolve rapidly in to the reticule.

The history of the bag is also determined by its changing contents. Some items remain constant from the late eighteenth and early nine-teenth century: money (in a purse), cosmetics, keys, handkerchief, diary, note pad and pencil, even printed literature such as the novel or commercial pocket book. Others have disappeared: the needle-work nécessaire (for no one sits sewing in company any more), the visiting-card case, for it is now integrated into the wallet, and the letter-case, as telephones and E-mail have replaced the art of letter writing. Fans are no longer fashionable because of regulated heating,

Plate 1 opposite Purple crocodile-effect leather handbag with metal clasp, bearing Treacy logo. British, 1998. By Philip Treacy. Top milliner Philip Treacy produced his first collection of handbags in 1997.
T.8–1999

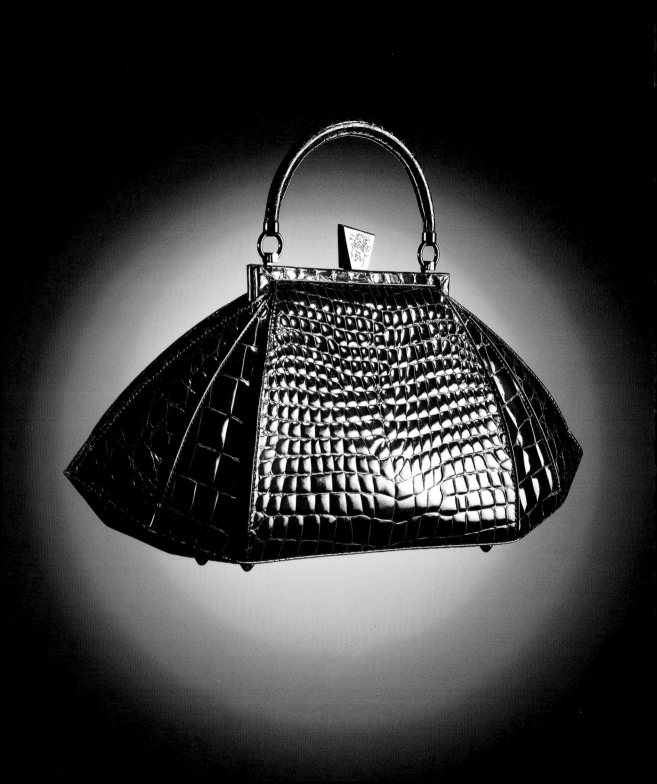

neither are smelling salts because of better hygiene. Additions in the late nineteenth and early twentieth century include a great increase in the range of cosmetics and, with it, the sub-genre of the vanity bag, smoking accessories, banking material and, since the 1970s, electronic aids such as the calculator, mobile phone and lap-top computer.

As containers of what is essential and important to women, so the bag is connected to the history of their lives, and what handbags

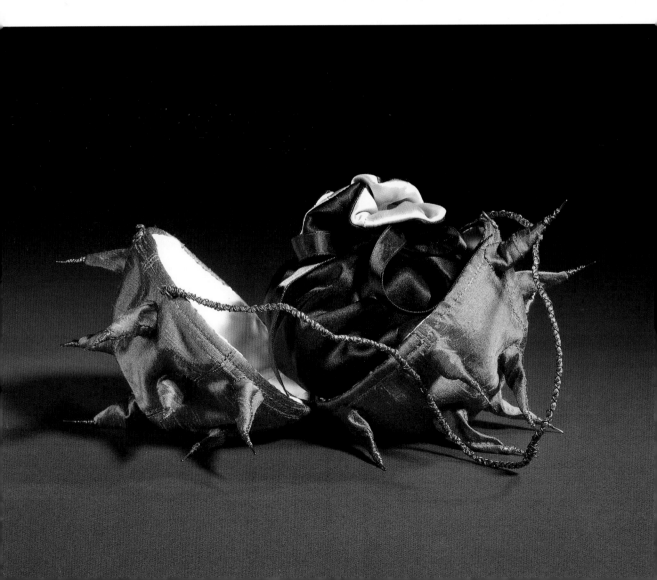

contain is personal and concealed. There have been exceptions: thimble, purse and perfume, amongst other desirable and expensive trinkets, were sometimes worn like charms at the waist. Transparent 'dance' bags of the 1950s were an extrovert's dream, while in the 1990s, Prada, one of the most desirable names in handbag design, produced a minimalist see-through bag – only the matching purse was coyly opaque. From Chanel there were clear-glass boxes, complete with chain strap and logo. Like an aquarium or shop-front window, nothing is more enticing than a peep into another world. Show is integral to fashion yet the handbag manages to be both display and secrecy, public and private, signifier and concealer. It is this dual function that gives the handbag such potent appeal, especially to dress and cultural historians.

Dress has always reflected affluence and aspirations, and accessories are vital indicators of style because of their ability to transmute more quickly, unlike expensive investments in clothing. The fashionable handbag has remained a stubbornly female accessory, mainly because of the existence of numerous pockets in men's wear, although the 1970s' shoulder bag and later backpack are androgynous items. It seems, though, that carrying a receptacle in the hand is innately feminine. Handbags remain, as they have done for the last century, highly significant items in a woman's wardrobe. Although certainly influenced by fashion, they are also personalised by the way in which they are used, becoming a projection of an individual. Many women have begun to subdivide their possessions into different bags: holdalls, briefcases for work and small shoulder bags for day, baby-changing bags and tote shopping bags and even recently a revival of the evening bag as jewellery. Perhaps such variety reflects the many sides to women's lives; it may even express contradictory sexual identities, as Alison Lurie suggests in *The Language of Clothes* (1982).

The handbag as we understand it today is an item that only became current in the 1880s. As an accessory that can embody luxury, be a practical friend or an expressive social tool, a crafted object or highly fashionable status symbol, it mirrors the spirit of the times as accurately as any article of dress. A small but powerful accompaniment to the ever changing lives of women, it has truly made itself 'indispensable'.

Plate 2 opposite 'Horse chestnut' bag with brown silk 'conker' purse. Green-silk dupion with copper wire British, 1996. By Emily Jo Gibbs. T.531:1+2–1996

Chapter One

Girdle Pouches and Almoners:

The Fourteenth and Fifteenth Century

These tournaments are attended by many ladies of the first rank and greatest beauty...their girdles are handsomely ornamented with gold and silver and they wear short swords or daggers before them in pouches, a little below the navel. (Henry Knighton, a description of a tournament, 1348: Cunnington 1952, p.77)

The early history of the purse is inextricably linked to the girdle, so important to medieval dress. The girdle was a cord or fabric band that hung loosely around the waist, gathering in the fashionably flowing robes of the time. 'Knightly girdles', worn only by the nobility, were made of ornamented, linked-metal sections, and were carried lower, round the hips. By the fifteenth century, women's girdles had become increasingly deep and ornate, and even constricting. The most expensive were made of patterned silk and had ornate metal buckles and ends. Both decorative and functional objects were suspended from the girdle (a common practice by women in later centuries). From the medieval girdle hung such items as a 'pair of beads' (or rosary), a Book of Hours, a pomander, the purse or almoner and, occasionally, a dagger.

Girdles and purses were important in the fourteenth and fifteenth century not only for their fashionable and functional assets but also for their symbolic qualities. In 1493–4, in *Le Parement et Triumphes des Dames,* Olivier de la Marche wrote a detailed treatise on the moral attributes of the fashionable lady's ensemble (Ribeiro 1986). This was a familiar fifteenth-century conceit, and he described in detail each item of clothing with its symbolic trait, from the chemise, which represented honesty, to the girdle, which represented virtue. The lavishly embroidered and jewelled purse embodied liberality and generosity.

Fig. 1 opposite This detail from a brass rubbing of W. Wyddowsonn and wife clearly shows her drawstring purse which hangs on a long cord from the waist girdle, and which is decorated with tassels. English 1513. Mickleham, Surrey.

E.521–1914

Even today it remains traditional to enclose a small coin in a purse given as a gift, to bring good fortune.

Very few bags survive from the medieval period, although many visual references to them exist in manuscript illuminations, such as the fourteenth-century Luttrell Psalter, portraits, carved effigies and tomb brasses in churches (fig. 1). Receptacles for small items and money, however, have always been necessary, and purses were an important part of fashionable secular dress for both men and women during the thirteenth and fourteenth century, for there were no pockets. Pouches were worn principally by men. Also known as pockets, purses or simply bags, they were worn at the centre or the side of the waist belt. They were made in soft leather or cloth and usually closed with a flap (plate 3); some were flat like pockets, others full and gathered (fig. 3), and they were slotted or sewn on to the belt for extra security. As an alternative the liripipe, a long extension on the chaperon (fabric hat) worn by men, was sometimes used as a purse, money being knotted at the end, while the Bagpipe Sleeve, which was very wide, could also be used to form a hanging bag.

Purses were also associated with marriage. A small group of French purses, which may have been betrothal gifts, have survived, now in the Musée de Cluny, Paris, the Musée des Tissus, Lyons, and the treasury of Troyes Cathedral. Depicted on them in fresh and delightful detail are the elegant men and women who appeared in courtly romances such as the *Roman de la Rose*. Just as the literature of chivalry mentions embroidery frequently, so the embroidered and woven bags use scenes from the poems and stories of the time. They depict tender lovers and charming monsters amid sinuous trees and flowers. The Museum fur Kunst unde Gewerbe in Hamburg has a drawstring linen purse with silk tassels embroidered in silk and gold thread, which was made in Paris *circa* 1340. It depicts two graceful lovers standing amongst trees, while the Provinciaal Museum voor Religieuze Kunst, Sint-Truiden, The Netherlands, has a small tapestry-woven purse with two fashionably dressed, crowned figures gesturing towards each other with outstretched arms. Betrothal purses were popular well into the seventeenth century and were given by groom to bride, representing the gift of the groom's wealth; they were some-

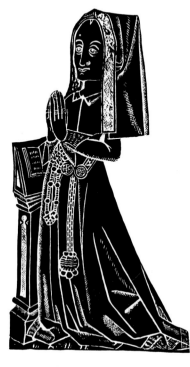

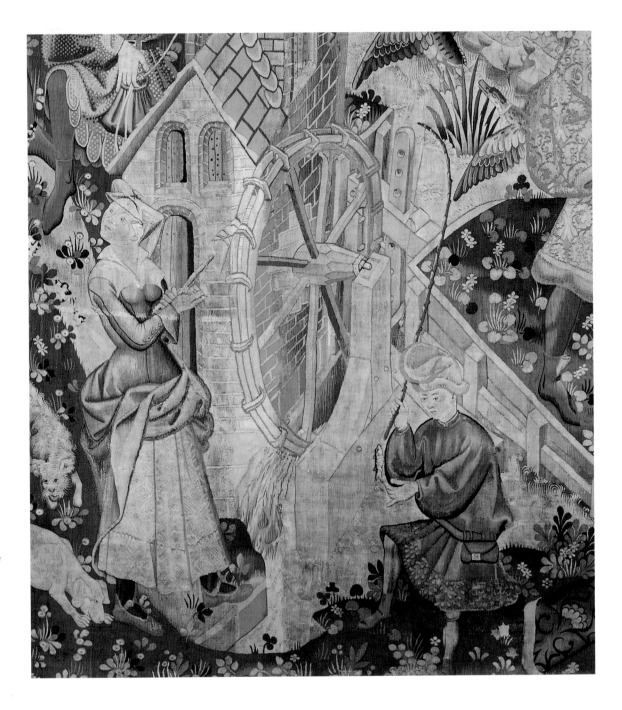

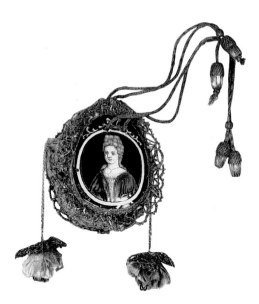

Plate 3 opposite Detail from *Falconry,* one of four Flemish tapestries collectively known as the Devonshire Hunting Tapestries. Flemish, mid-15th century. The man wears a waist belt with a soft leather pouch that closes with a flap. T.202–1957

Fig. 2 above Limoges marriage purse of pink silk with silver lace and enamelled miniatures of a couple. French *c.*1680. (For a similar example, see Foster 1982, p.18.) 2042–1855

times given to wedding guests as well. The French town of Limoges was famous for its betrothal purses; the V&A has a fine example with an enamelled portrait of a betrothed couple attached to either side (fig. 2). The hollow interior of the purse may have also had an association with fecundity; filling it with money further emphasised the hope for a successful marriage based on prosperity and fruitfulness.

Another more formal type of purse associated with marriage is one that bears heraldic emblems. Some were made from woven silk patterned with heraldic devices; a thirteenth-century silk purse, woven in Spain, was found in a medieval ditch in London in the early 1900s and features castles, fleurs-de-lis and swans (Egan and Pritchard 1991). The Calthorpe Purse, *circa* 1540, one of the earliest purses in the V&A (plate 4), was probably made for the marriage of Sir Henry Parker, Knight of the Bath, to Elizabeth, daughter and heir of Sir Philip Calthorpe of Suffolk, and second cousin to Anne Boleyn. The purse is formed of four panels in a shield shape, each embroidered in tent stitch on linen with the marshalled arms of the family alliances.

Ornate and delicate drawstring purses were favoured by well-to-do women, and these were known in the fourteenth century as 'hamondeys'; many were made of woven or embroidered silk with metal thread, of velvet or linen, or of embroidered leather, sometimes dyed red with madder. Most were gathered with strings and embellished with tassels and usually worn on the right of the girdle buckle.

In the Middle Ages, the French town of Caen was famous for its rich purses, known as 'tasques', but the fashion for embroidered or woven drawstring purses is thought to have derived from the East; in some thirteenth-century Guild papers of Paris reference is made to the 'makers of Saracen purses' (Bridgeman and Drury 1978). By the end of the Middle Ages, the trade in mass-produced accessories included belts and purses of silk and precious metal, which were brought from the towns into the country by itinerant tradesman. Pawnbrokers' inventories of the time often mention purses and girdles, many of them a combination of fabric and precious metals, and it has been suggested that they may have been bought as investments (Pipponier and Mane 1997, p.88).

Transporting money and precious objects in attractive bags on the

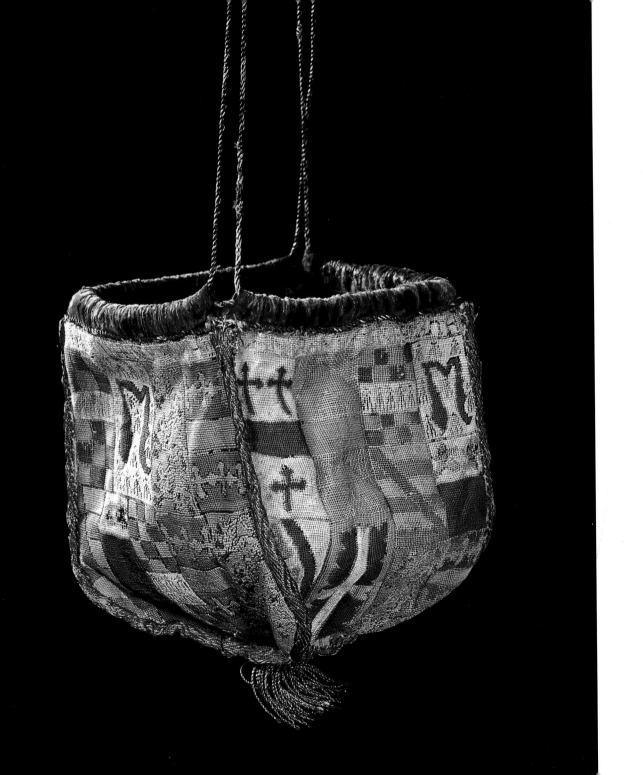

body, with banking in its infancy, carried an element of risk, and one of the earliest-known references to the 'cutpurse' came in 1362. Valuable purses also began to be worn by the middle classes. In the *Canterbury Tales* of the late fourteenth century (Robinson 1974, line 3250), Chaucer describes the carpenter's wife's outfit; her everyday bag is embellished, a sign of money to spare:

And by hir girdel heeng a purs of lether
Tasseled with silk and perled with latoun.

Soft leather or fabric bags, over-sewn on to a metal frame with a top fastening, were used in Anglo-Saxon times and became popular again in the fourteenth and fifteenth century. Like the girdle pouch they also hung from the girdle, and some were used as game bags, perhaps to hold food for a pet falcon; these were known as *charnières* in France. A few early examples survive, including a fourteenth-century brass semicircular frame (without its fabric), which was found in excavations on the Thames shoreline. Two elaborate fifteenth-century 'escarcelles'– or purses for secular use – one of cut velvet, one of leather, with curved, iron frames and ornate clasps shaped like castles, are in the collection of the Metropolitan Museum, New York.

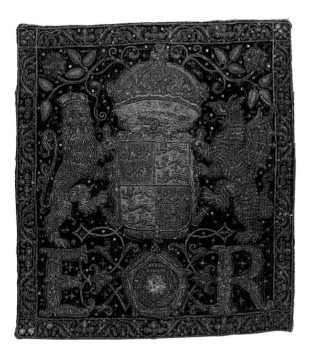

Burses, as ecclesiastical purses were known, had great significance. Many survive, kept in cathedrals (such as in Troyes) and abbeys in France. Some were, as today, to collect the offerings of the congregation in church, suspended from a straight metal carrying handle and often richly worked. Others were used to contain relics or to hold corporals – linen cloth used in the celebration of the mass, and these tended to be drawstring purses. Purses were also used to contain symbols of state and government. These were richly ornamented with embroidery, jewels and gold. Most important of these was the Seal Bag, made for each successive Keeper of the Great Seal, later known as the Lord Chancellor. Burses or purses made to contain the Great Seal were sometimes made from old vestments but more often were especially richly embroidered. The sixteenth-century burse illustrated in fig. 4 bears the Royal coat of arms, worked in gold and silver thread on crimson velvet in raised and couched work. As an accessory to ceremonial dress, its tone is regal and formal, in keeping with its official nature.

Fig. 4 above Embroidered burse for the State Seal, bearing the Royal Arms. English, 1560–1600.
T.40–1986

Fig. 5 opposite Purse with gilt and chiselled-iron mount and velvet body, made in the Renaissance style (*c.*1600). Probably French, 1880s.
M.120–1921

Chapter Two

Pokes, Purses and Swete Bagges:
The Sixteenth and Seventeenth Century

A purse of blewe silke and golde.

(Nichols New Year's Gifts to Queen Mary, 1556: Cunnington, 1964, p.185)

In the early sixteenth century, women wore pouches suspended at the waist on strings and made of soft leather, velvet, 'tynsel', satin or, more luxuriously, cloth of silver or gold. Such a 'bage' is described in 1510 in Lincoln Wills: 'A tany [tawny] bage with knoppys [tassels] off gold and strynkes off grene sylke' (Cunnington 1964, p.86).

Other bags and purses were naturally more workaday: in Albrecht Dürer's drawing of *A Nuremberg Woman in Indoor Dress* (Albertine, Vienna), drawn in 1500 of an informal outfit of a Nuremberg house-wife, possibly using his wife Agnes Frey as a model, a large pouchlike bag is attached to the left side of the belt. The pouch closes with draw-strings but also has smaller drawstring purses attached to it, similar to a reproduction purse in the V&A (fig. 5).

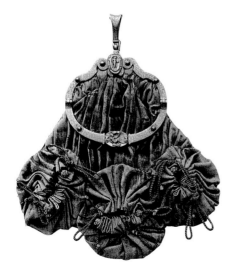

Large, satchel-like leather or cloth bags were worn diagonally across the body by peasants and travellers. We know this from artists who depicted working people, such as Peter Breughel the Elder's *Two Peasants* (mid-sixteenth century, illustrated in Boucher 1966, plate 539), and from images of St James, patron saint of pilgrims, where he is always shown carrying a large shoulder bag or purse. The most humble articles of all have tended to disappear – for recycling was not unknown in the sixteenth century. 'I have a pair of worsted stockens, the legs of them I pray you to get me a purse, a large one, made of them with a lock ring. I will have the fringe that shall go about it to be of silk' (Cunnington 1954, p.146).

As fashions in men's and women's dress changed and styles grew fuller around the hips so large girdle pouches went out of fashion, replaced for men from the mid-sixteenth century by pockets made of soft leather, set into the sides of breeches. Women began to carry small bags that hung on very long tasselled drawstrings, concealed amongst the folds of the skirts.

Despite the introduction of pockets, men continued to carry drawstring purses of worsted wool, leather, or even silk or metal thread. Some were ring or peg knitted, employing a disc of wood with a central hole surrounded by wooden pegs, which was used to form a knitted tube. Most were of an elongated shape and fastening with rings at either end (predating the misers' purses of the eighteenth and nineteenth century), and were looped over the belt or tucked away in the clothes. Sometimes the wearer could not remember where, 'Which made them feel where their purses were, either in sleeve, hose or at girdle' (Cunnington 1964, p.146).

Swete Bagges

One gross of Crimsen Sarsenet swete Bagges and viij lb of swete powder as well to make swete our Robes and apparell. (An order to Adam Bland from the Tower of London, 1562: Arnold 1988, p.232).

In an age when sanitation and hygiene left much to be desired, disguising unpleasant odours was a part of aristocratic life. Many personal items were perfumed, from handkerchiefs to gloves, and lavender bags are recorded in inventories as far back as the fourteenth century. Just as pomanders had been hung from the girdle in the fifteenth century, so 'swete Bagges' filled the air around the person with a pleasant perfume as well as providing a disinfectant effect. The bags were filled with powder made from sweet-smelling herbs and spices or perfumed wads of cotton. In the early seventeenth century these included such delights as 'damaske powder fyne' made from rose petals, 'muske Civett', 'amber gryse', lavender and ground orrisroot, which smelt similar to violets. Sweet purses were used in the storage of clothes and linen in chests for the same reasons, as well as to deter vermin. It remains common to place lavender bags amongst sheets and pillowcases.

The Seventeenth Century

For his purse … lay in the sleeve of his doublet … A fair new purse with white
strings and great tassels … [he] thrust it into the slop of his hose, as he was
wont, letting the strings thereof hang out for a traine. (S. Rowlands, *Greene's
Ghost:* Cunnington 1955, p.78)

Purses were small in the first half of the seventeenth century. Some
were shaped from two pieces of fabric in a square or oblong, which
closed with double drawstrings and were embellished with tassels.
Others were rounded with a curved metal frame that closed with a
latch or 'snap-hance' (plate 5). While many purses that survive were
made by professional workshops, some appear to be domestic work;
these are sometimes dated, intended perhaps as a gift, bearing a
message, name or monogram (plate 6).

The most luxurious embroidered purses, made in leather, velvet
and silk, were used by both men and women. Men carried theirs in
sleeves, pockets or hose, and the plainest, such as peg-knitted purses,
were worn at the belt. Women's purses were similar to those carried

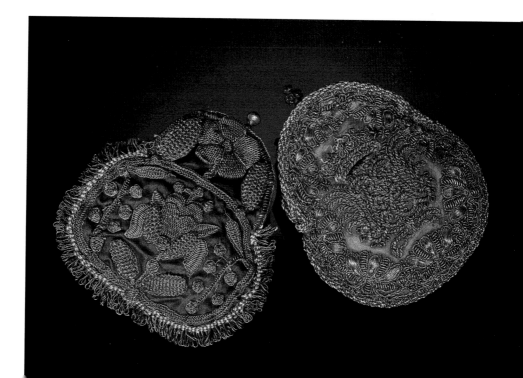

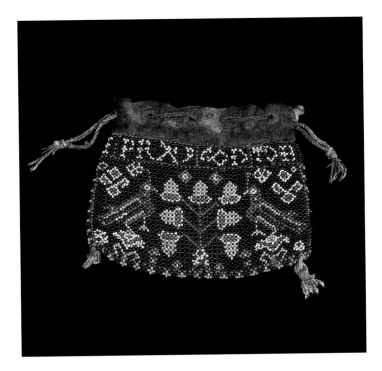

by men, but smaller, taking the form of tasselled bags that closed with tasselled drawstrings. These were often embroidered, while bead-work on leather was also popular (plate 6).

Purses were not only used to contain money and personal trinkets, they were also used as decorative containers for gifts such as money, perfume or jewels, and although the transaction was often a public one, the items contained remained private. Gifts were exchanged between friends and given to royalty at the New Year, and these were recorded in great detail. The purse itself was not an inconsiderable part of the cost of the gift, and for this reason was often described in contemporary accounts: 'By the Earle of Darbye in a purse of crymsen satten, embraudered with golde, in dimy soveraignes ... 20.0.0' was a New Year Gift to Queen Elizabeth in 1561 (Pamela Clabburn, 1978, p.218). In the Earl of Bedford's Accounts for January 1660 there was 'Presented to the Lord Chamberlain in gold for the King – £20; for an embroidered silk and silver purse ... 9s'.

Plate 6 above Drawstring leather purse embroidered with glass beads. English, 1634. A sprig of green and yellow acorns appears between a pair of birds with lozenges and flowers, inscribed 'I PRAY GOD TO B(sic) MY GUIDE 1634'. T.55–1927

Fig. 6 opposite Purse or sweetmeat bag, made of engraved mother-of-pearl incorporating two Tudor roses with silk lining, with plaited drawstring and loop handle. English, early 17th century. T.197–1966

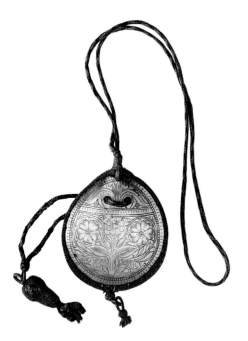

Purses are also associated with the lighter side of life in the sixteenth and seventeenth century, in particular with gambling and cards, which was enjoyed by both men and women. Gaming purses were specifically functional. Made with a circular, stiffened base, the gathered sides were formed from a narrow circle of cloth such as velvet, which released to form an open container for coins or gaming chips; many were monogrammed to ensure that takings were claimed by their rightful owners (plate 7). Purses were associated with saving as well as spending, and this was sometimes alluded to in their decoration. Embroidered or beaded purses in the seventeenth century often included acorns in their pattern (plate 6), an exhortation perhaps to 'save and prosper', as Vanda Foster points out in *Bags and Purses* (1982). An early seventeenth-century purse (plate 8) is made from a single nutshell, covered with embroidery and lined and hinged with silk. Barely large enough to contain a few coins, the purse was probably a novelty gift, but its maker may also have had the thought in mind that large oaks grow from tiny acorns. In the same genre, the V&A has a tiny purse or sweetmeat bag, made of engraved mother-of-pearl and silk, with plaited silk drawstrings (fig. 6). Many early seventeenth-century purses are in very good condition, suggesting that they were valued keepsakes, such as a tiny bunch of grapes, exquisitely embroidered in the finest detail and lined with silk (plate 8), while a small group of purses and matching pincushions show no evidence of pin marks at all, but may have been hung from the waist of aristocratic ladies to be seen rather than used (plate 9).

Seventeenth-century Embroidered Purses

Embroidery was 'the taste, fashion and fancy of the day' (Wingfield Digby 1963, p.23). Its widespread contribution to the cultural and social manners of Tudor and Elizabethan times was partly a result of the stability of the contemporary economic conditions. Embroidery skills were taught to young girls as a part of their domestic education and played an integral part in everyday life. Embroidery also provided a living for numerous professional embroiderers who worked to commission. Many of the embroidery projects of the great houses would have been impossible without their involvement. The anonymous

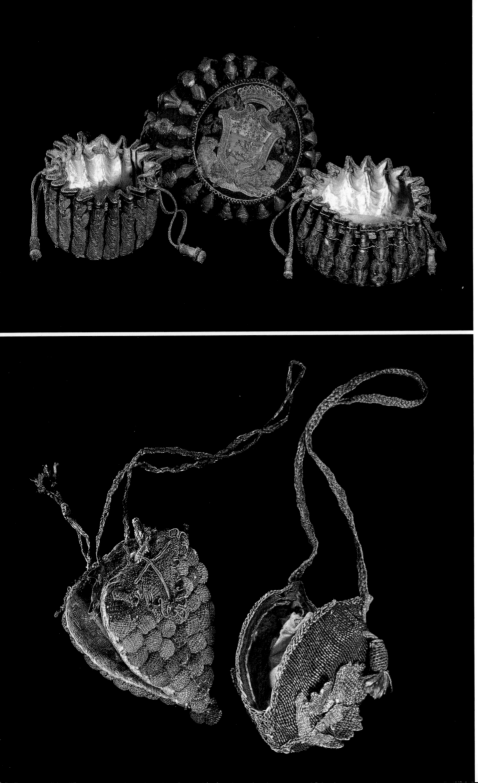

Plate 7 left Group of crimson and green velvet gaming bags, embroidered with gold and silver thread, two with coats of arms on the base. French, 1600s. The bags open to form shallow containers for coins or counters. T.20–1939; 522–1869; 4062–1856

Plate 8 below Two tiny purses. Left: linen embroidered with coloured silks, silver-gilt and silver thread and pearls, with padded buttonhole stitch and tasselled cords. English, mid-17th century. T.172–1921 Right: two halves of a large walnut shell covered in green silk and worked in detached buttonhole stitch over silver thread and braid stitch. Lined with green silk, which forms the inner purse, with plaited silk drawstrings. English, first half of the 17th century. T.57–1978

Plate 9 opposite Embroidered purse with matching pincushion, English, 1600–50. Silver and silver-gilt thread and coloured silk, in tent and braid stitches, in a design of birds amongst floral sprays. T.52&A–1954

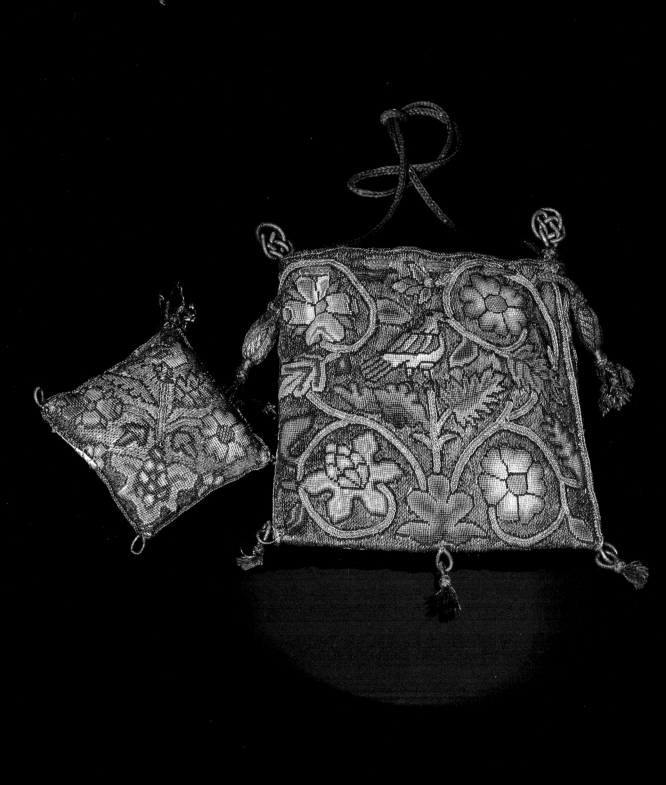

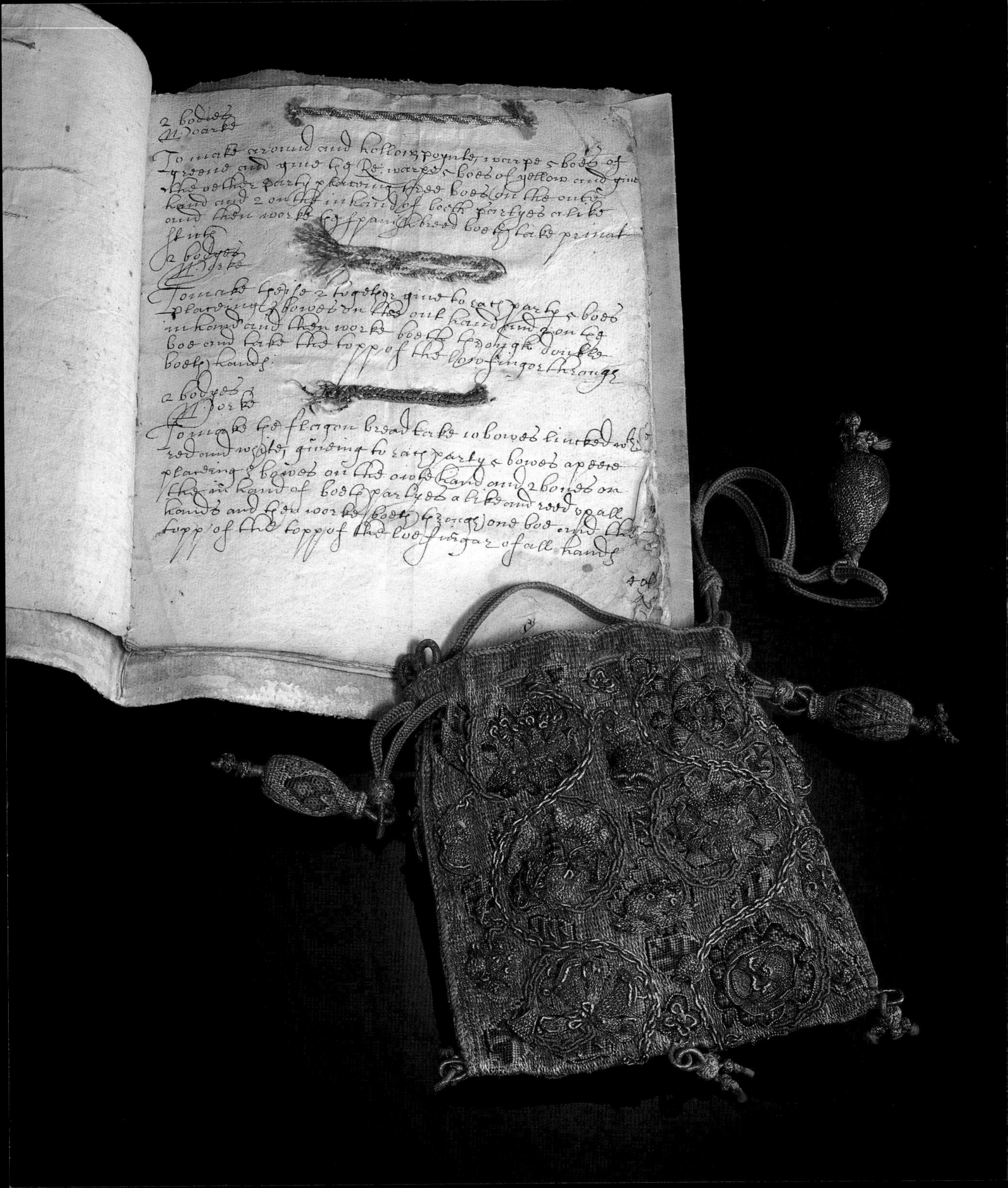

2 bodies
Woork

To make around and hollow poyntes, warpe 5 boos of
greene and gius her Re warpe a boos of yellow and gius
the other party a turning thre boos on the out
hand and 2 on the inhand of boeth partyes alike
and then woork her spangld bred boos her take pricat

Stuck
2 bodies
Woorke

To make house 2 together gius to each party 5 boos
placing her 2 boos on the out hand and on her
boos and then woork boos through dowble
boose hands

2 bodies
Woork

To make her flagon bread take 10 bowes turned with
red and white, giueing to each party 5 bowes a pece
the inhand of boeth partyes alike in red up all
hands and then woork boos through one boo and the
topp of the topp of the loo finger of all hands

Plate 10 opposite
Manuscript book with
instructions for plaiting
cords and purse strings, with
samples worked in coloured
silks and metal threads.
English, *c.*1600. T.313–1960
Embroidered purse of canvas
with coloured silks, silver
and silver-gilt thread with
plaited silk strings similar
to those shown in the
manuscript book. English
*c.*1600–1625. T.127–1992

Fig. 7 below Purse worked
in needle lace in coloured,
silver-gilt and silver thread.
English *c.*1700. The two
pairs of figures were
worked separately and then
incorporated with the green
ground. T.198–1927

play *Sir Giles Goosecap* (1606), described the work of one such embroiderer: 'He will work you any flower to the life, as like delicate perfumer, he will give it you his perfect and natural savour … He will make you flies and worms of all sorts, most lively'.

In the seventeenth century, needle-lace and embroidery patterns were disseminated through pattern books such as *The Needle's Excellency* published by James Boler (1631): 'A new book wherein are divers Admirable Workes wrought with the Needle. Newly invented and cut in copper for the pleasure and profit of the Induftrious'. The pattern was dusted through the designs' perforations on to the fabric with 'pounce', chalk or powdered charcoal, or drawn freehand. A rare manuscript book of purse-string designs survives in the V&A (plate 10). Many seventeenth-century embroidered purses have also been kept, prized for the liveliness of their embroidery and tiny scale. These were valued later by Edwardian collectors, such as Lord Lever, who formed large collections of sixteenth- and seventeenth-century embroidery (plate 11).

The Late Seventeenth Century

Towards the end of the seventeenth century, purse styles in England became increasingly more sophisticated. Their form changed from a simple drawstring to more complex shapes, and they used a greater variety of materials (plate 13). Knotting and netting became popular, tassels became larger. The illustrated needle-lace purse (fig. 7) reflects the interest in chinoiserie of the late seventeenth century. Many woven purses were made in France, some as marriage gifts (plate 13). Typical of these styles are silk- and metal-thread tapestry-woven purses, formed from four shield-shaped panels with naturalistic, pictorial scenes, such as that illustrated (plate 12), with its fine detail of ships at sea. A similar tiny doll's purse, about one and a half inch square (belonging to the late seventeenth-century Lord and Lady Clapham dolls and now in the V&A), is made of blue damask brocaded in cherry-

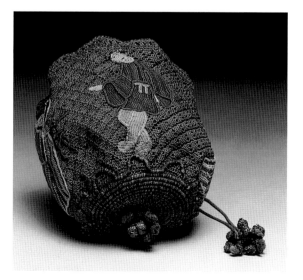

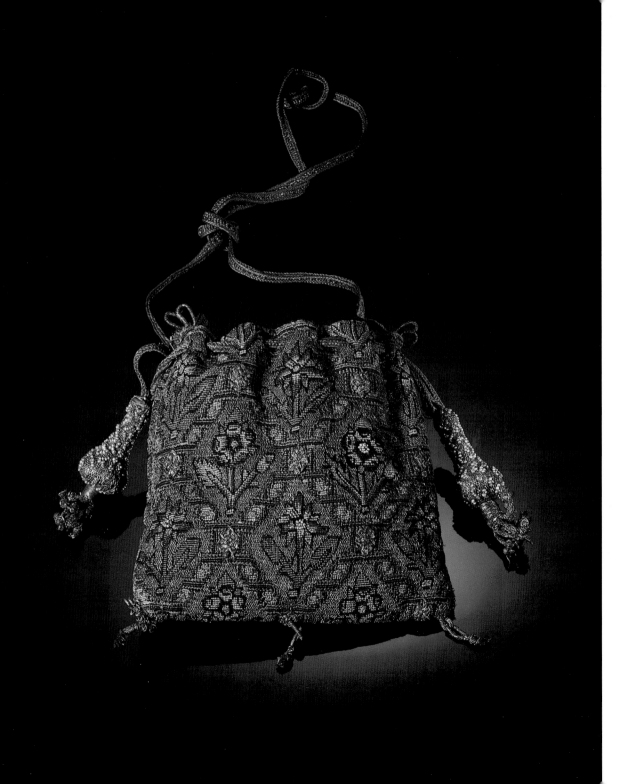

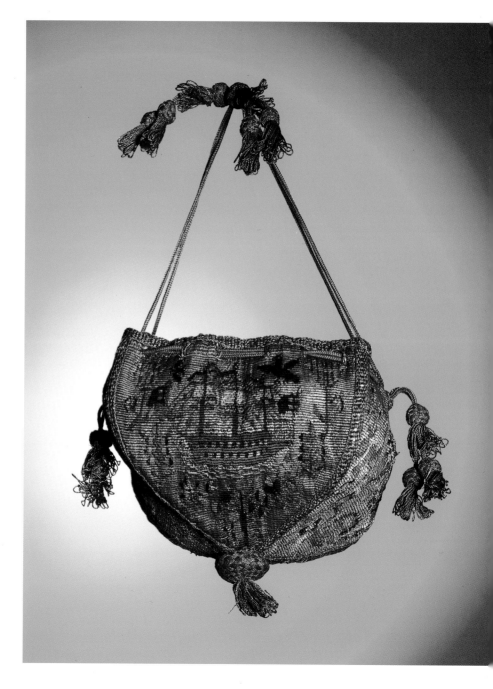

Plate 11 opposite
Embroidered purse with
silver and silver-gilt thread,
seed pearls and coloured
silks forming a pattern of
flower sprays and a lozenge
diaper. English, 1st half of
17th century. The drawstring
is silk braid with large
tassels trimmed with pearls.
T.53–1954

Plate 12 right Tapestry-
woven silk and silver thread
purse, possibly French or
Northern European, 1600s.
Consists of four panels with
a sailing ship surrounded by
birds, stags, an oak and a
fruit tree, birds and flowering
plants including variegated
tulips. 552–1901

colour silk and silver thread, the pattern large in proportion to the tiny scale of the bag. The fabric was probably French, *circa* 1690–5, and could have cost as much as £2.10s a yard, being material of the highest quality. Lord and Lady Clapham form a precise document of fashions of the late seventeenth century, and it is delightful that the bag survives as it is not attached to the dolls. It has four shield-shape panels, braided seams with plaited-silk drawstring and silver bobbles, and contains two tiny silver pennies, which are later in date. Seventeenth-century purses and work-bags form part of a lively group of secular embroidery, and superb quality examples survive, both from the domestic and the professional workshop.

Plate 13 below Tapestry-woven purse of silk and metal thread in a Cupid and heart design with a green silk ribbon trimming formed in loops, with tassels, possibly associated with marriage. French, late 17th century. The quotation AQUILAURA, formed in a mirror image, is French and in full reads *c'est a qui l'aura* (it is a question of who gets it first). 557–1893

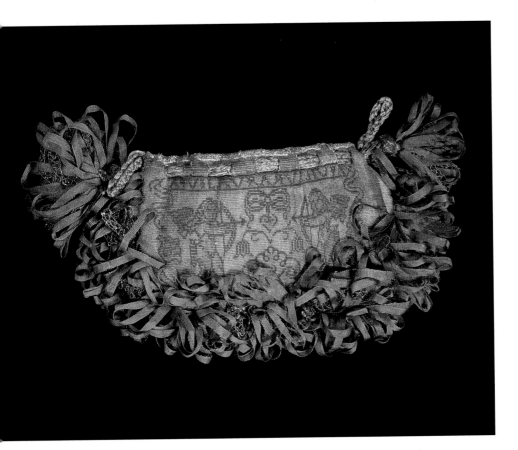

Chapter Three

Pockets, Purses and Work-bags: 1700–1790

At the same time he gave Mrs Jenkins an Indian purse, made of silk grass, containing twenty crown pieces. (Humphrey Clinker, *Tobias Smollett,* 1771: Penguin edition, 1967, p.390; see plate 24)

For most of the eighteenth century women's skirts were generously full and capacious pockets were worn, hidden amongst the folds of fabric. Small purses were also used throughout the century, held in the hand, looped over the waist or kept in the pocket, and their manufacture played a significant role in domestic embroidery of the day. Large drawstring work-bags were integral to leisured women's lives, reflecting the importance of domestic needlework. The emergence of the reticule towards the end of the century developed in part from the work-bag, as women had already begun to take advantage of its capacity to hold a fan or purse. By the late eighteenth-century, some form of bag had become essential, for as Neo-classical, closely fitting styles came into vogue, they rendered pockets unattractive and reticules necessary.

Pockets

All the money I have … I keep in my pocket, ty'd about my
middle, next to my smock.
(Jonathan Swift, Mrs Harris' Petition, 1701: Cunnington 1957, p.178)

Pockets were separate articles from skirts in the late seventeenth and eighteenth century. Flat and pear-shaped, they were usually made in joined pairs and tied around the waist with tapes, sitting on the hips over the petticoat and reached through side slits or placket holes in the skirts. Pockets were functional: deep and roomy and made of

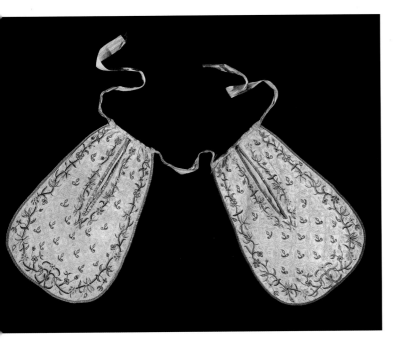

stout materials such as linen or dimity, a cotton fabric with a raised stripe, and lined for extra strength with a central, vertical opening bound at the edges. Most pockets were for personal use or presented as gifts, and many were dated and initialled. A shopping list of 1741 included: 'Coloured dimothy for pockitts, buckram, canvas, tape, thread' (Cunnington 1957, p.178). Many were beautifully embroidered with coloured silks in delicate floral patterns (plate 14), or worked with hard-wearing wools, flame stitch being particularly popular. Pockets were worn by all classes of society, and with respective varia- tion in quality. Pamela, in Samuel Richardson's eponymous novel of 1740, received, like most servants, gifts of clothes from her employers. She acknowledged that some were above her station, saying, 'Here ... are a pair of pockets; they are too fine for me, but I have no worse' (Everyman Library edition 1978, vol.I, p.65).

Despite being beautifully worked, pockets were personal items, not seen by strangers except when stolen by a skilful thief, as observed in Francis Coventry's novel of 1751, *Pompey the Little,* in a widely quoted

Plate 14 above Pair of linen tie pockets, embroidered in coloured silks in chain stitch. English 1700s.
T.281&A–1910

passage: 'My chief dexterity was in robbing the ladies. There is a peculiar delicacy required in whipping one's hand up a lady's petticoats and carrying off her pockets'. The eighteenth-century lady's pocket contained many of the essentials of her daily life: money and keys, cosmetics and perfume, various needlework tools when they were not in a work-bag and a folding fan. Following Lady Isham's death in 1667 it was recollected that 'Her ample pockets abounded with dainty implements' (Groves 1966, p.42).

Pocket Cases

It was a most beautiful pocket case, the outside white sattin work'd with gold, and ornamented with gold spangles; ... it is lined with pink sattin, and contains a knife, sizsars, pencle, rule, compas and bodkin, and more than I can say; but it is all gold and mother of pearl. (Groves 1966, p.64)

The pocket also gave its name to some other portable accessories such as the pocket book or pocket case and to the pocket-handkerchief, although the latter, by now a fashionable accessory, was carried in the hand. The pocket case described above, a gift to Mrs Delany from Queen Charlotte in 1779, was exceptionally luxurious, but richly decorated pocket and letter cases were part of the oeuvre of eighteenth-century domestic embroidery. These were often made in silk, and beautifully embroidered (plate 15) with silk or silk ribbon and metal threads; some had silver-gilt fringes, strings and tassels, others were signed and dated (plate 17). Smaller pocket cases were used as card holders in France and were embellished with flirtatious mottoes or conundrums. Larger versions with divided pockets were used for letters, bank bills and documents of value, and perhaps a piece of felt employed as a pen wiper or a square of fabric for pins and needles. Later eighteenth-century examples often featured embroidered medallions with a central image such as a silhouette or cornucopia, or incorporated a plaited lock of hair, indicating that it may have been a gift of particular intimacy. Folding leather letter cases were sometimes brought back as souvenirs by travellers or given as gifts by foreign envoys. Many originate from Constantinople and some bear dates and monograms (plate 17).

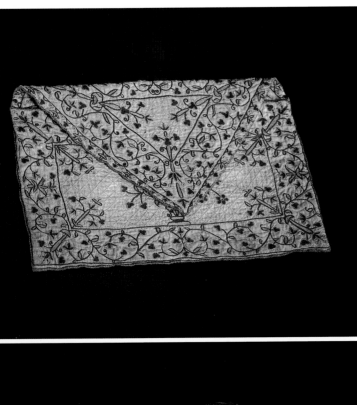

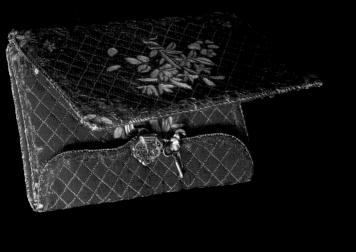

Plate 15 top left Silk pocket case, or pocket-book cover, in an envelope shape with tiny flower sprigs worked in coloured silks. British, 1750–75. Circ.238-1926

Plate 16 below left Silk pocket case, embroidered with coloured silks and silver-gilt thread. French *c.*1750. The oval panel is painted in watercolours, with similar panels inside, and possibly refers to a Royal marriage. 1937–1899

Plate 17 opposite Two wallets, or letter cases, from Constantinople. Turkish. Left: wallet embroidered with silks and metal threads on silk, dated 1748, and embroidered CONSTANTINOPLE. Right: brown leather folding wallet with four sections, embroidered with fine silver-and-gold metal thread and green silk; inscribed in gold thread: SR WILLIAM PORTMAN, CONSTANTINOPLE 1682. T.115–1992; T.40–1987

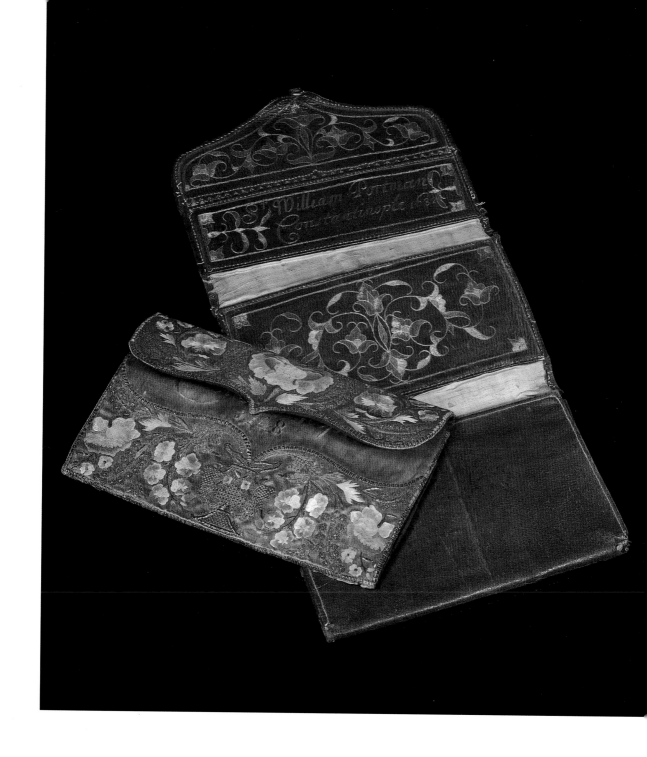

Pocket Books

I dressed it myself from a print in *The Ladies Memorandum Book* for the last year. (Oliver Goldsmith, *She Stoops to Conquer,* 1773)

Pocket books differed from pocket and letter cases. They were small, leather-bound, commercially printed manuals that were produced in great numbers in the second half of the eighteenth century. The forerunner of the women's magazine of the nineteenth century, they were printed yearly and bore titles such as *The Ladies Most Elegant and Convenient Pocket Book* or *The Cabinet of Fashion and Ladies Pocket Companion.* Pocket books were not only carried in the pocket but also functioned as a receptacle. Many contained a pocket for note book and pencil between the printed manual and its leather case, and were closed securely with metal fastenings. Women also personalised them, as, carried about for a whole year, they became familiar companions in which to store vital snippets of fabric, letters and even bank bills amongst their pages.

The printed contents of the pocket book included a calendar, diary pages, columns for accounts, hackney-carriage rates, 'Feasts, Fasts and Holidays throughout the Year', recipes, puzzles and 'favourite new songs', and much more. Of great value to dress historians, they also included information on the latest fashions. Pocket books were sold widely in the provinces as well as the major towns, which made them invaluable vehicles for the dissemination of fashion, despite the fashion engravings being printed retrospectively. Barbara Johnson's Album of Fashions and Fabrics, which is in the V&A's Textiles and Dress Collection, was compiled between 1746 and 1823 and provides a unique record of one well-to-do lady's sartorial history. It contains samples of fabric of her outfits and their cost, as well as many engravings of fashion plates from pocket books of the time (Barbara Johnson facsimile edn, ed. Rothstein 1987, T.219-1973).

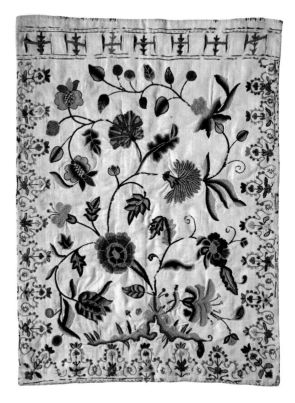

Plate 18 below Drawstring work-bag embroidered with coloured wools. British, 1712. T.205–1970

Work-bags and Knotting Bags

Meanwhile, to heighten all her charms
The work-bag dangled on her arms;
The very bag that British Belles
Bear on their arms at Tunbridge Wells
(*The London Magazine, or Gentleman's Monthly
Intelligencer,* 1764: Cunnington, 1957, p.399)

Capacious work-bags were an important domestic accessory in the eighteenth century, and their decoration and scale reflected changing fashions in needlework, although their form – two squares of fabric seamed at the base and sides and closing with a simple drawstring – remained plain. Late seventeenth- and early eighteenth-century work-bags tended to be large, to contain the substantial hanks of coloured worsted wool used for crewelwork, and made of linen or cotton. Many were embroidered with crewelwork, typically with twisting Tree of Life patterns, complete with foliage and birds such as that illustrated (plate 18), which is dated 1712. Various sewing implements, often highly decorative, were contained in much smaller bags or rolls and stored in the pocket or work-bag. For the first half of the eighteenth century, these were also suspended from the girdle or waist belt on a metal châtelaine, or ornamental chain. Girdles were often made from a narrow ribbon with a buckle, such as that mentioned in the *Weekly Journal* in 1731, 'a gold and silver girdle with buckles set in Bristol stones' (Cunnington 1957, p.143). Many small accessories such as cosmetics and jewellery, mirrors, patch boxes, perfume bottles and watches were also suspended to decorative effect from the châtelaine, while less fancy items were kept in the pocket. The practice of keeping many of the essential needlework tools about the person continued until the rigid, compartmentalised sewing casket developed in the late eighteenth century, following the development of the reticule, which replaced the pocket. Work boxes, or caskets, became available by the end of the century in all types of materials and quality, from wood to tortoiseshell or papier-mâché. Many were inlaid or painted and were fitted out with fine sewing implements in silver, ivory or mother-of-pearl, with writing quills and scent bottles.

Up until this point, home-made needlework bags were much appreciated gifts, especially when they were made with affection. A diminutive flowered silk bag, made for her friend and later sister-in-law Martha Lloyd by Jane Austen in the early 1790s, when she was 17, contained 'minikin' needles and thread, and a tiny pocket with a note penned in miniature script:

This little bag, I hope will prove
　To be not vainly made;
For should you thread and needles want,
　It will afford you aid.

And, as we are about to part,
　'Twill serve another end:
For when you look upon this bag,
　You'll recollect your friend.

Knotting in silk or metal thread first became fashionable in the late seventeenth century, the technique probably brought over from China, and from the 1760s small, lightweight-silk drawstring knotting bags emerged, replacing the heavy linen crewelwork bags. They were used to hold the silk, cotton, woollen or linen thread and small shuttle needed for knotting. Knotting produced a narrow trimming with raised knots, or *picots,* at regular intervals. This was applied to small objects or fabric as part of its pattern or, alternatively, short lengths were attached to braid to make fringing. Jane Austen's nephew Frank was fond of knotting curtain fringes.

The small oval shuttles that were used in knotting provided an opportunity for decoration and were made in a great variety of materials: mother-of-pearl, tortoiseshell, cut steel, amber or ivory; they were contained in small, beautifully embroidered bags. Some were valuable, as in the case of 'a gold knotting shuttle of most exquisite workmanship and taste' (Groves 1966, p.86), given to Mrs Delany by George III in 1783; Madame de Pompadour was given a gold shuttle with enamelled branches with jewelled cherries, which cost 550 livre, an enormous sum at the time (Groves 1966, p.87). Lost shuttles featured regularly in newspaper advertisements, such as one placed in the 1760s that described, lost 'a gold coloured shuttle, filled with gold covered silk thread, in a bag of rose coloured taffeta embroidered with silver'. As this illustrates, knotting bags were also themselves highly ornamental. Some were made of dress remnants, worn to match a dress, others of embroidered silk, or beribboned and trimmed with knotted fringes. Knotting bags proved too tempting not to use for other things, despite the continuing existence of pockets. In her journal for 27 October 1769 Lady Mary Coke describes an amusing incident *(Letters and Journals 1756–74):*

An English Lady, by her Affectation of french airs, amused me extremely ... She swam into the room, as She fancy'd, perfectly *à la Mode de Paris,* but I, who have been there, saw her only *à la Mode de Lyon.* She was painted up to her ears & had a knoting bag hanging to her arm. She began her conversation with saying She was very glad they permitted one at Paris to wear embroider'd knotting bags, for when they were obliged to be the same with one's Clothes, it was very troublesome, 'tho' indeed,' said She, 'I never knott, but the bag is convenient for one's gloves & fan'.

Knotting was a graceful occupation and did not require a great deal of concentration. It was frequently pursued in public, both when visiting and in the more public domain; ladies were even seen knotting at the Opera in 1770, as observed by Lady Mary Coke (Ribeiro 1986, p.113). This was particularly the case in France, where knotting was known as *La Frivolité,* carried in beautiful, large, silk drawstring bags, beribboned and fringed. One aspect of knotting in public was that it reflected well upon the maker. In *The Dictionary of Court Ceremonial* (Groves 1966, p.86), written by Madame de Genlis, the shuttle is defined by its womanly, graceful, symbolic qualities 'expressing the aversion which all females ought to have to complete idleness'. The importance of the knotting bag is reflected by the many portraits of fashionable ladies in the eighteenth century who are portrayed in the act of knotting, the fullness of their ornate silk bags reflecting that of their skirts (fig. 8). While such industry was desirable to provide for items of household linen or dress, as a social occupation needlework also symbolised dutiful, feminine activity and in addition proved pleasing to the eye, perhaps drawn to the graceful movements of the hand.

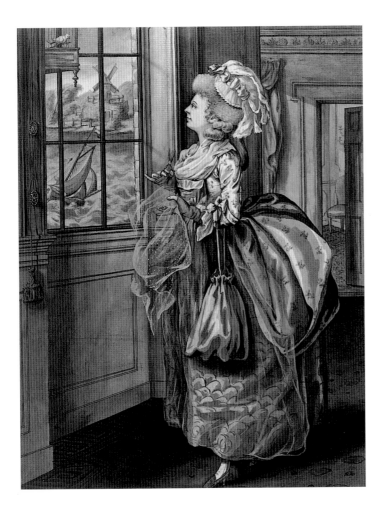

Other developments in domestic needlework affected the design of work-bags. The vogue for 'parfilage', or unravelling precious silver and gold threads, developed in elevated social circles during the late eighteenth century. It positively amounted to a craze, particularly in the French Court where the 'parfileuses' spent many hours stripping out-of-date embroidered garments, furnishings and trimmings, and selling them to goldsmiths for not insignificant sums. Such enthusiasm soon gave rise to specialist, highly decorated implements such as scissors, a knife and a sharp point for unpicking, contained in special

Fig. 8 above Watercolour of a woman with a large drawstring work-bag over one arm, holding a pair of scissors and a piece of spotted-silk gauze. Gauze was very popular and expensive, and she may be making either an apron or a kerchief. British, *c.*1780. By Robert Dighton. E.35–1947

Plate 19 opposite Finely beaded purse, with the inscription IAME MON ESCLAVAGE and ICY EST MON SECRET. French 1700s. Bearing the monogram and motto of Marie Antoinette, the purse may have been associated with her or her court circle. T.168–1992

cases or small embroidered bags or purses, with which large bags were filled with untwisted gold. The fashion spread to England, brought over by dispossessed French aristocrats. 'Drizzling', as it was known in England, remained a domestic rather than courtly occupation, lasting into the nineteenth century. In England, drizzling bags were provided in the great houses for discarded items of metal threadwork, and precious embroideries were completely destroyed.

Purses

Many workshops in early eighteenth-century France produced small purses, a speciality being those embroidered with pearls, and many were exported abroad. The finest French work was in beadwork, in particular the sablé-worked, drawstring purses and wallets of the mid-eighteenth century, so finely beaded they resembled grains of sand (plate 19). These were made in specialist workshops in Paris using up to 1000 per square inch of extremely small and fine glass Bohemian and Venetian beads, the production of which had recently become technically possible. Many commemorative purses were made to mark special royal occasions, wars or personal events. The craze for ballooning in the early 1780s, following one of the first successful

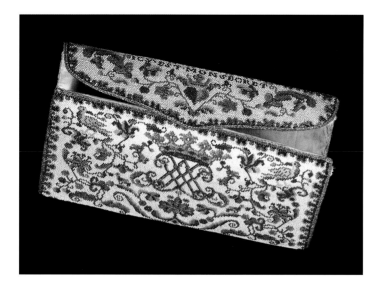

ascents in 1783, resulted in many textile designs featuring balloons as part of the pattern. The same motifs were also seen in French beaded purses of the time.

Home embroidery and beadwork was less sophisticated, although by the standards of today beautifully accomplished (plate 20). *The Lady's Magazine* included patterns for pockets and purses from the 1770s, which could be attached to ready-made, top-closing metal frames, many of pinchbeck, an imitation gold, or other metals (plate 21). Before this, designs were copied from professionally designed patterns

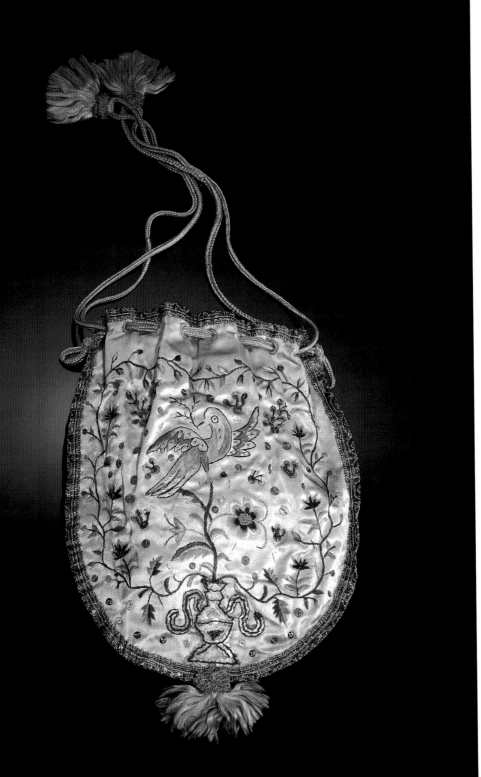

Plate 20 opposite
Embroidered bag or pocket
with matching muff (not
shown). The bag shows the
transition between hidden
pocket and external reticule.
Although embroidered for
show and with drawstrings,
the bag still resembles a
pocket. British, second half
of 18th century. T.724C–1913

Fig. 9 below Wooden purse
stretcher and moulds.
Left: purse mould or 'moule
turc' for peg-knitting, used to
'knit' a long tube from which
purses were formed.
Centre: stretcher for shaping
and stretching netted wallet
purses. Right: thimble-
shaped mould used for
working buttonhole stitch
purses. British, 19th
century. T.59-5–1925

or existing work. Beads were often used in conjunction with other techniques, to highlight parts of a knitted pattern or to form a solid base for soft purses. Very fine, multicoloured bead knitting was popular for purses, in which there was a single bead for every stitch, producing a dense beaded surface (plate 22). Purse moulds (fig. 9) were hollow cup shapes around which a purse was worked with needle and silk or metal thread, using a simple open buttonhole stitch that could also incorporate beads. The purse once removed from the mould could be lined and was closed with a drawstring. From the early eighteenth century, fine steel needles were used to knit purses and small bags in patterned silk, and their workmanship was very fine (plates 23 and 33). A small number of machine-knitted purses also began to become available.

Ribbon purses were briefly popular in the eighteenth century, made from lengths of coloured-silk ribbon that was interwoven over a thin square mould to form simple geometric patterns. The ribbon was then cut and finished and a drawstring added. Light, and too delicate for outdoor or heavy use, ribbon purses were used to contain money for games or cards, or as small needle-and-pin holders, while for visiting, small needlework cases were carried in ribboned bags, often more for decorative than functional effect.

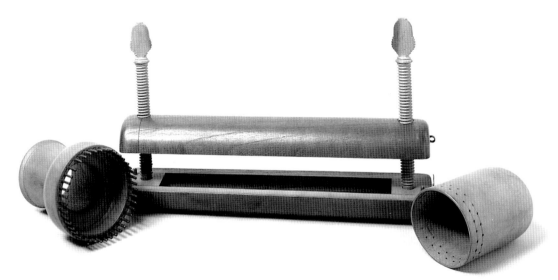

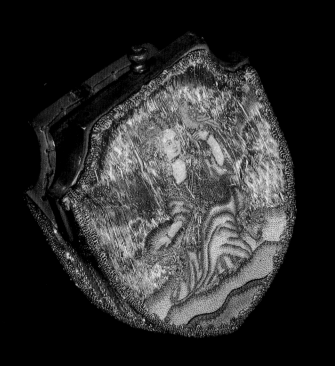

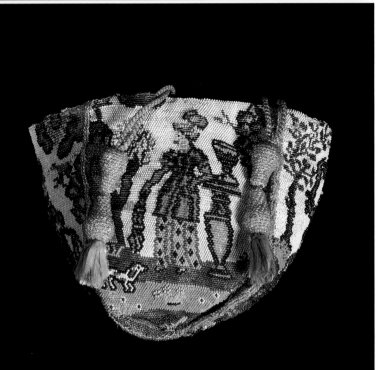

Plate 21 top left
Embroidered purse with two
flat shield-shaped sides.
French, 1700s. One side
has a figure in classical
dress seated on a couch
with a globe and dividers,
the other has a figure
holding a parrot. The purse
has a metal mount. T.89–1935

Plate 22 below left Brightly
beaded purse made in
four sections, each bearing
an allegorical figure, one
representing Justice, with
pink silk cords and tassels.
French, 1700s. T.321–1965

Plate 23 opposite Left: silk
and gold thread netted
purse, with hinged gilt frame.
British, 19th century.
T.29–1946 Right: knitted silk
purse, with gilt opening bars
and finger-ring. British, late
18th century. T.257–1922

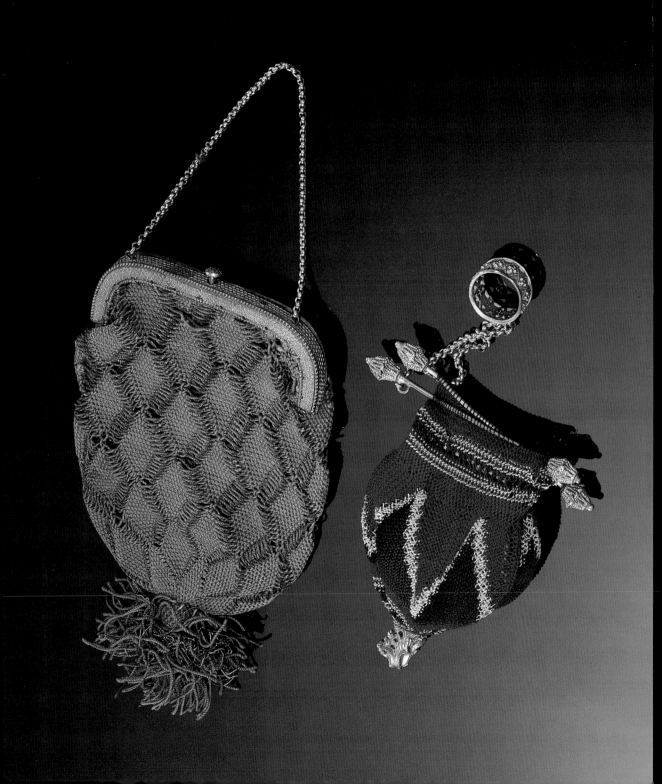

Netted Purses

Netting became popular in the second half of the eighteenth century and continued into the early nineteenth; practised by both men and women, the most well-known product was the netted purse (plate 24). Catherine Hutton wrote in *Reminiscences of a Gentlewoman of the Last Century* (1891): 'I have worked embroidery on muslin, satin and canvas and netted upwards of one hundred wallet purses ... I net much still'; see plate 23. Netting was done mainly with silk, linen, cotton or woollen thread and was used to make a variety of small- and large-scale objects in a fine or coarse openwork net. It was done with the aid of a netting box, sometimes known as a purse-netting box, which contained gauges for different size mesh and shuttles, and a small roller to wind on the work. Betsy Sheridan, sister of the playwright Richard Sheridan, bought a netting box in 1785 for her sister: 'There is a box for you to put your netting in while you work it, and to keep it in when you are idle, with lock and key' (Groves 1966, p.81). Many different objects were netted; at the end of the eighteenth century some women netted garments, while Jane Austen's nephews 'amuse themselves very comfortably in the even'g – by netting; they are each about a rabbit net'.

Netting was used to create many thousands of stocking purses, the most popular style of the eighteenth and nineteenth century. Many have survived and are known also as misers' or wallet purses. Women carried them held in the middle, letting them fall elegantly to either side of the hand, while men put them in their pockets. The majority of stocking purses were netted, although some were knitted, or later crocheted. They were often worked with geometric patterns or bands, embellished with beads or silver- or gold-foil strip or with narrow silk ribbons woven through the mesh. Once worked, the elongated tube of netting was put on an expandable purse stretcher to shape it (fig. 9). It was then sewn up with small weighted tassels at either end and squeezed through a pair of silver or cut-steel rings, known as 'sliders', which were used either side of the central opening slit to secure and separate the different coins stored at either end. Specialist shops such as Thomas Gardom of St James's Street provided the necessary materials – 'Purse-Twist, Tassels and Sliders of all Sorts'

Plate 24 opposite Netted bag made of bast or another plant fibre, with tassels. English or French, *c*.1760. T.428–1966

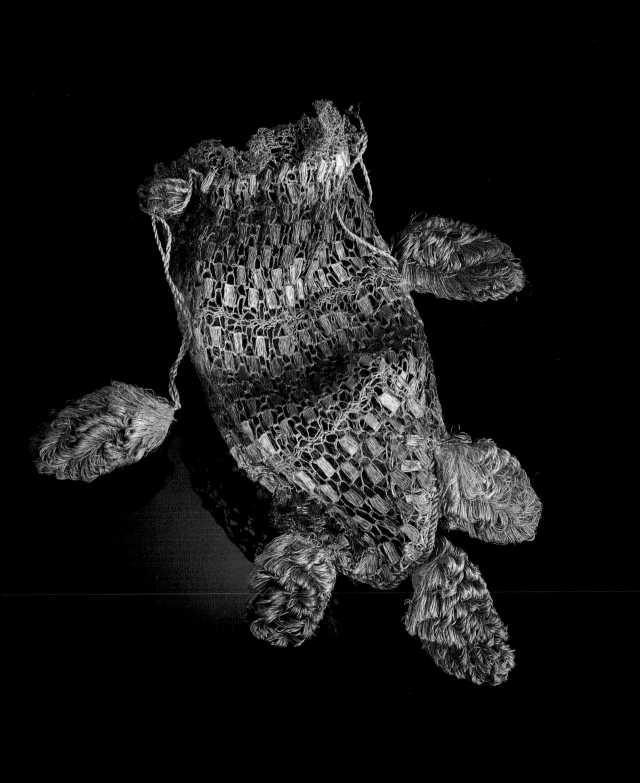

(Foster 1982, p.24). Towards the end of the eighteenth century stocking purses became large – some 17 inch or longer – and could be tucked over the belt. Many netted purses were made as presents for gentlemen, and green, the colour of love, was popular. Rather too many were made in some cases – Lord Bessborough wrote to Sarah Ponsonby: 'I desire the favour of you not to send me the Purse you mention, for I have, I believe, twenty by me which are not of any use' (Foster 1982, p.19).

Netting became so popular that supplies of thread sometimes ran out in the country. Jane Austen wrote in October 1798 that Mrs Ryder's shop had 'scarcely any netting silk; but Miss Wood, as usual, is going to town very soon, and will lay in a fresh stock'. She wrote to her sister Cassandra in 1799: 'You quite abash me by your progress in netting, for I am still without silk. You should get me some in town or in Canterbury; it should be finer than yours' (Byrde 1979, p.31).

Commercially Made Purses

Purses were sold by travelling merchants and pedlars, who not only took clothes, fabrics and accessories beyond London and Paris but also spread fashionable changes to the provinces. In William Hogarth's engraving *An Election: Canvassing for Votes* (*circa* 1754), a Tory candidate buys a purse from a Jewish pedlar for some girls leaning through a balcony window. Country women, unschooled but with an interest in fashion, relied on travelling merchants. Hannah Wainwright, who died in 1734, left her nieces various items including two gold rings, two silver thimbles and a purse 'wrought with silver' (Buck 1980, p.133). In Paris and London, shops stocked full with goods developed rapidly in locations such as Ludgate Hill, Oxford Street and the Royal Exchange, a fashionable market with stalls selling expensive merchandise, jewellery and other fashionable and tempting goods. In addition, milliners, haberdashers, fancy-goods stores and perfumers also sold purses.

Fig. 10 opposite 'Parisian Ladies in their Winter Dress for 1800', *Fuchs Die Frau in Karikatur.* Coloured illustration between pp 296 and 297. In their clinging and semi-transparent gowns, the fashionable figures carry large reticules, circular or pentagon-shaped, hanging to the knee on long handles. NAL

Chapter Four

Reticules: 1790–1830

While men wear their hands in their pockets so grand,
The ladies have pockets to wear in their hand.
(*The Imperial Weekly Gazette,* 1804: Cunnington 1959, p.369)

In the 1790s the fashionable silhouette became elongated, replacing the earlier full skirts with a simple, unadorned look inspired by Grecian styles. These Neo-classical styles originated from post-Revolutionary Paris, approved by the Consulate as appropriate to the new regime. Plain muslins and cambric (a very fine white linen) were favoured, replacing the rich brocades of the eighteenth century. Skirts, falling in columnar lines from a high waist, clung to the body, especially as the number of underclothes were gradually reduced (fig. 10). Elizabeth Austen was shocked by an officer's wife's lack of stays and bare bosom at a dance in Ipswich and wrote to a friend on 16 February 1798 that 'Such a mode of dress or undress would be remarked even in London so that you may judge what an uproar it makes in a Country Town' (Tomalin 1997, p.129). The waist was now far too high for bulky pockets, for, as the *Chester Chronicle* of 1796 explained: 'The Ladies' waists have ascended to the shoulders'. For a while, the balantine, an external pocket that hung from the high waistline, was tried but proved unpopular as it interfered with the elegant lines of the skirts. Women were left with the problem of where to carry purses and fans. In S. Mercier's New Picture of Paris, written following his attendance at a public ball in the French capital in the winter of 1794–5,

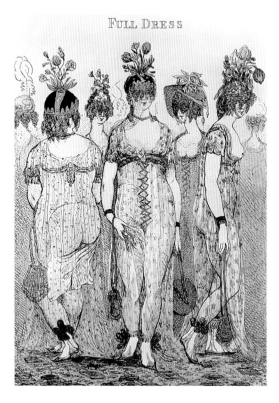

FULL DRESS

shortly after the Reign of Terror, he describes the event with great immediacy, perhaps borne of shock (Ribeiro 1986, p.124):

Here lighted lustres reflect their splendour on beauties dressed à la Cléopâtre, à la Diane, à la Psyche ... bare arms, naked breasts, feet shod with sandals, hair turned in tresses around their heads by modish hairdressers, who study the antique busts. Guess where are the pockets of these dancers? They have none; they stick their fan in their belt, and lodge in their bosom a slight purse of morocco leather in which are a few spare guineas.

Knotting and work-bags had already begun to be used for fans and purses, as *The Times* noticed, rather late, in 1799: 'The total abjuration of the female pocket. Every fashionable fair carries her purse in her work bag ... the new custom of carrying a bag with her handkerchief, smelling-bottle, purse etc' (Cunnington 1957, p.399). By this time, it could be argued that what the reviewer had really seen was a reticule. In France these were initially known as ridicules, and they were soon carried by every fashionable lady. There were various different styles for different occasions. *The Journal des Dames et des Modes* spoke of

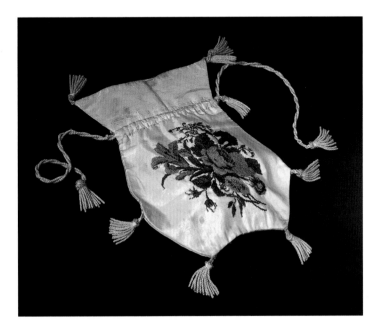

Plate 25 opposite Flat, hexagonal-shaped silk reticule with floral embroidery and silk cord tassels. British, 1800–24.
Circ.554–1954

Fig. 11 below Fashion plate published by Vernor Hood & Sharpe Poultry, 1 November 1807. Shows 'full dress' and trapezoid-shaped reticule, possibly supported on a boned or wired frame.
E.2594–1888

'*des ridicules du matin, des ridicules de sociétés, des ridicules de bals, des ridicules de spectacles*'. In England, the 'ridicule' became a focus of satirists and cartoonists, for the vagaries of fashion often provided materials for the general entertainment of their readers. Although British women took longer to embrace the idea, they soon came to rely on them, and called them their 'indispensables'. An English magazine *The Gallery of Fashion* (1 November 1799) had to explain that 'Indispensables are bags, which the ladies use instead of pockets'.

By the turn of the century, high-waisted Directoire fashions had become firmly established and were to continue to dominate for the first two decades of the nineteenth century. The banishment of the pocket inspired one of the richest periods of development in hand-held accessories, as a great diversity of reticules (as they later became known) and purses in various materials and styles appeared. Their usefulness and decorative qualities were enjoyed to the full, and, despite the later reintroduction of pockets, reticules, once gained, were hard to relinquish.

Reticules: 1800–1821

The 'indispensable' was so new that in 1801 the press recorded: 'A number of disputes having arisen in the *Beau Monde* respecting the exact position of ladies' indispensables (or new invented pockets)' (Cunnington 1938, p.73). The indispensible was fast becoming an essential fashion item, as the slim lines of French Directoire fashion continued to preclude the wearing of pockets. Drawing on all the accumulated technical and artistic skills of the eighteenth century, reticule styles bloomed in the early years of the nineteenth century (fig. 11).

Large round, hexagonal or lozenge shapes (plate 25), based on the military sabretache of the Napoleonic Wars (1799–1815), were favoured (Foster 1982). Their flat sides provided a vehicle for embroidered, beaded, painted and applied decoration, which often featured various Neo-classical, architectural and floral motifs. Some were soft, others had round, stiffened bases, while further variants were based on novelties, such as a pineapple-shaped reticules (*circa* 1800, Kyoto Costume Institute, Japan), worked in silk crochet. Some were fringed

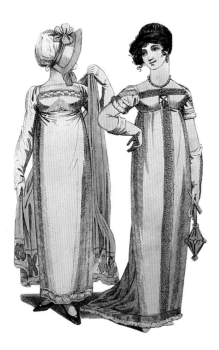

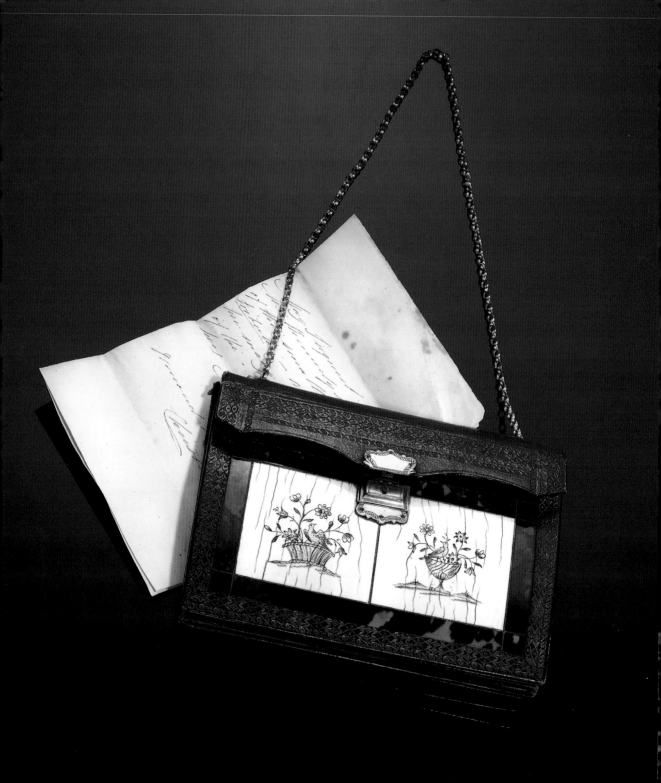

or tasselled, made of finely embroidered silk taffeta scattered with tiny flowers, sprigs, butterflies, birds, trailing ribbon-bow motifs or Neo-classical medallions, or sometimes with a central motif, such as an urn, a basket of fruit or a cornucopia of flowers, framed by an embroidered wreath. Edgings were made of lace or metallic lacework, with sparkling sequins. Satin with chenille became popular, and velvet painted with flowers and classical architecture.

The simplicity and plain, light colours of dress fabrics gave accessories an added aesthetic importance that went beyond that of function, and the reticules made in the first quarter of the nineteenth century are both inventive and delightful. The effect of the decoration was all the more striking for being seen against the plain backdrop of the high-waisted skirts, for fashions favoured plain, light colours or small, delicate prints. The long strings by which reticules were often carried, held delicately by the fingertips or wound gracefully around the wrist, served to emphasise the elegant Neo-classicism of fashionable dress. Achieving a fashionable look became possible for a wider social range of women as less expensive materials were favoured. The sheer nature of these fabrics continued to cause comment. Instead of concealing the pocket, one commentator noted in 1803 that the dresses themselves could be contained in a pocket book: 'A dress may now be made so exceedingly fine and thin, that it may be carried in a pocket-book or conveyed by the two-penny post to any part of the town' (Bradfield 1968, p.86).

Amongst other things, the reticule might contain rouge and face powder in paper packets, fan, purse, scent bottle, card money, handkerchief and smelling salts. Towards the end of the eighteenth century, fashionable society adopted the custom of leaving visiting cards, and card cases soon became another item usefully contained by the reticule. Contemporary documentation is not limited to fashion plates or cartoons. Lord Melville's famous trial of 1806 is notable to the bag historian not for its legal implications but for the 'rows of pretty peeresses, who sat eating sandwiches from silk indispensables' (Foster 1982). Although there were strict codes of etiquette, social codes began to change in the late eighteenth century concerning physical contact, and many etiquette books were written in the nine-

Plate 26 opposite
Rectangular leather bag with flap and brass catch, stamped gilt border and panels of tortoiseshell surrounding two incised ivory panels. British, probably 1819. With gilt chain. Containing a letter with the watermark BATH 1819, addressed to Mrs Kennedy, Capel Street, which reads 'May I request My dear Mrs Kennedys acceptance of this small Christmas tribute – and wishing you many happy returns of the day. I remain very very affectionately M. Hamilton Christmas Day'.
T.85–1968

teenth century. As society changed, so the maintenance of the social order became ever more important in what C. Willet Cunnington (1938, p.3) called 'the rising tide of democracy'. Shaking hands with women became acceptable, after a suitable introduction, in certain circumstances and always with gloved hands. The relationship between bag and gloved hand became an aesthetic one, imbued with flirtatious power. In 1810, the *Morning Herald* (Cunnington 1959, p.381) wrote: 'Though it is not the mode for ladies to wear pockets in public ... no gentleman would refuse to take hold of the lady's ridicule while she is dancing.'

For a while, matching a reticule to the outfit was popular – many were made of dress fabric by dressmakers. The magazine *Le Beau Monde* noted in 1807 that 'Indispensables are still much worn and of the same colour as the dress'. But this soon passed out of fashion for, in the same year, Mrs Calvert described the outfit of a rather unfashionable acquaintance in her Journals. 'She was a little squab figure ... her gown blue and a blue ridicule to match, dangling on her arm.' By 1811, ridicules of the same material as the pelisse were passing out of fashion for it was observed that: 'This article is considerably on the decline with females of a superior order' (Cunnington 1938, p.45).

Reticules continued to be made of fine materials, in sympathy with the lightweight dress fabrics of the period, and satin netted over with silk, shot silk, sarcenet and, later, velvet were popular. Floral embroidery in coloured silks and metal threads was prevalent, often incorporating raised work with shaded ribbons, gauze, straw and even human hair. Most were trimmed with tassels and closed with silk cords or ribbons. For outdoor wear, reticules began to become more substantial and rigid. Some were constructed with great ingenuity out of a variety of materials, such as papier-mâché and tortoiseshell. These required the additional skills of the metalsmith and leather-worker, and tended to be made commercially. The leather handbag was first introduced in about 1815 in the form of an envelope with a flap fastening and metal catch, rather similar to the eighteenth-century leather pocket book but with a handle. Many were ornamented with metal plaques, or tortoiseshell or ivory panels (plate 26). As waistlines began to drop back down to their natural level, stiffer dress fabrics

Plate 27 opposite Circular beadwork bag. British, 1820–50. Hinged metal clasp with imitation jewel insets and chain frame, and short looped fringe all around. T.28–1946

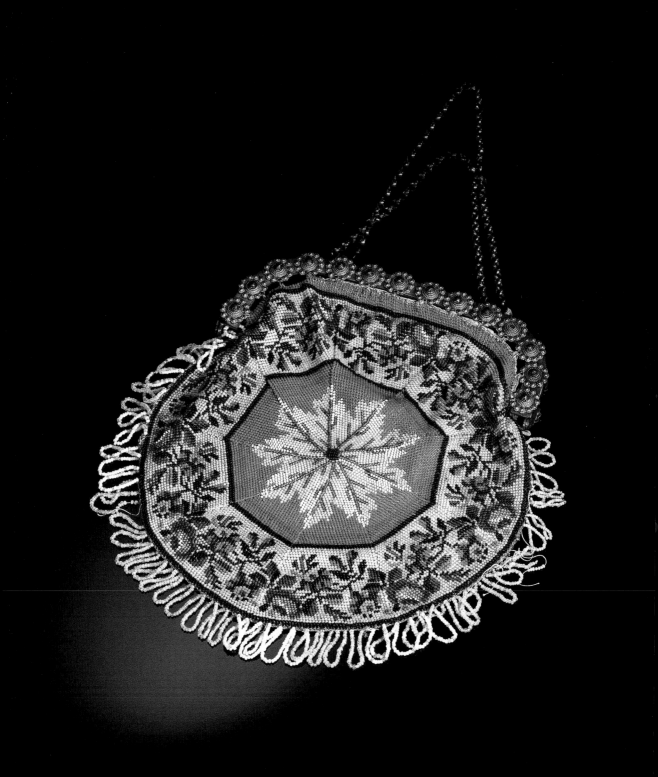

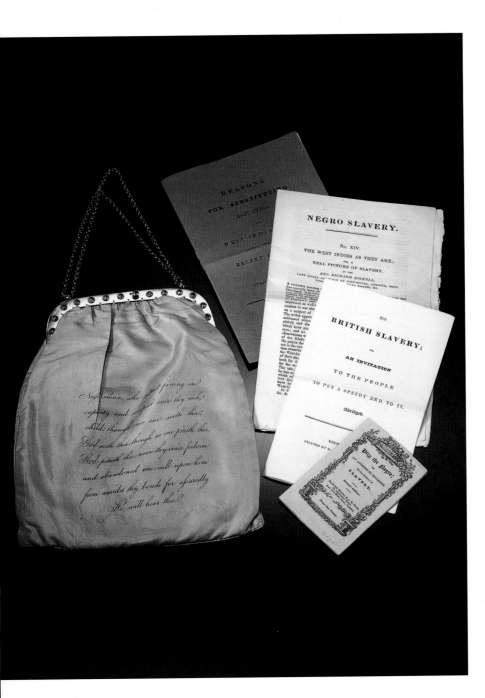

Plate 28 left Silk reticule with steel frame and chain with printed designs. British, 1827. On one side a black woman nurses a child in a tropical landscape, on the other is printed 'Negro Woman, who sittest pining in captivity and weepest over thy sick child: though no one seeth thee, God seeth thee; though no one pitieth thee, God pitieth thee; raise thy voice forlorn and abandoned one; call upon him from amidst thy bonds for assuredly He will hear thee'. Shown here with 1827 anti-slavery pamphlets printed in Birmingham and London. The bags may have been sold by the Ladies Society for the Relief of Negro Slaves, founded in 1825 in West Bromwich. T.20–1951

Plate 29 opposite Left: red velvet reticule with body of papier-mâché pressed in the shape of a scallop shell, metal chain and mount. British, 1820s (see Blum 1978, p.42) for a fashion plate by Ackermann's Repository, 1824, featuring a very similar reticule). T.449–1985 Right: handbag made from turquoise silk plush, with metal clasp and slide fastening and brackets for the padded handle. Pouch-shaped and made from a single piece of fabric with gussets. British, 1880s. T.215–1983

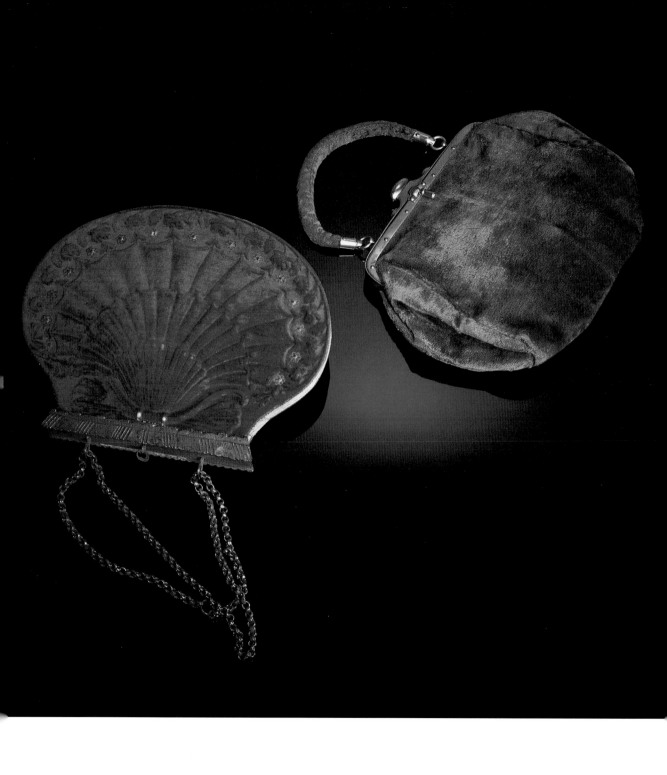

were favoured, which was reflected by a new substantiality in reticules, by 1818 being made in green velvet, blue satin and even cork.

Reticules: 1821–30

She trailed a reticule in her hand like a two-penny post bag.
(*The Hermit in London,* 1819: Cunnington 1959, p.381)

Between 1821 and 1830, fashions began to move rapidly away from the vertical, high-waisted style, towards a new romanticism and fullness. Reticules continued to be made of soft dress fabrics, their decoration becoming more ornate with fringing and floral motifs. In 1820, circular shapes closing with a drawstring of ribbon or cord were popular and easily made at home. Lightweight frames with silver or steel clasps (plate 27) and chain handles were available ready-made, and fabric bags were simply stitched on to them. One unusual group of bags bears abolitionist propaganda in support of the anti-slavery movement (plate 28).

Rigid shapes made from moulded papier-mâché or card overlaid with silk continued in forms such as a circle, a lyre or an urn, the two halves hinged with silk or kid, or with concertina sides. Others were made from kerseymere (a woollen twill), or red morocco. They were held by short handles and closed with tortoiseshell or cut-steel clasps. In 1822 tortoiseshell reticules became popular, with leather side folds. Reticules began to resemble the later handbag, in both construction and fastening. One popular shape was a moulded shell shape. An Ackermann's costume plate of 1824 (Blum 1978) shows a promenade dress with a shell-shaped reticule (plate 29). Reticules reflected the preoccupations of the fashionable silhouette quite literally sometimes. In an Ackermann plate of 1820 (fig.12) a day outfit is shown with a small, flat hexagonal shaped reticule with carrying handles, which fastens with a flap and clasp. The neatness and geometry of the reticule compliment the self-contained lines and plain skirts of the high-waisted fashions of the time, over-elaboration being confined to the bonnet.

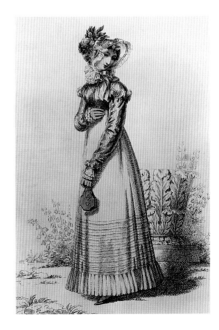

Chapter Five

Bags, Purses and Châtelaines: 1830–1880

As he talked on, he grew quite bold, and actually had the audacity to ask Rebecca for whom she was knitting the green silk purse? He was quite surprised and delighted at his own graceful familiar manner. 'For any one who wants a purse,' replied Miss Rebecca, looking at him in the most gentle winning way. (William Thackery, *Vanity Fair*, 1848: Penguin edition 1968, p.71)

Reticules: 1830–1850s

Developments in science and industry had an enormous impact upon fashion in the nineteenth century, and reticules and purses were increasingly made by machine from the 1830s. The expanding market for small goods was fuelled by demand from a society that was more and more able to take part in fashion. Shops and department stores flourished, selling many home-produced and imported goods to an ever widening market. In the 1830s the sentimental look that followed from the austerity of Neo-classical styles found flat, embroidered, fringed bags often with flap fastenings based on the envelope idea of the pocket book, secured with a small button and a silk-cord handle. Typical of this time was white satin embroidered with flowers worked in couched chenille threads, their petals made from fine cotton gauze and edged with silk fringing, while layering of sympathetic fabrics was popular. In the 1830s, the lozenge shape was still popular, made of coloured, beaded or hand-painted velvet. In 1834, in *Jorrock's Jaunts and Jollities* (Cunnington 1959, p.418), a lively girl is described out walking, 'on her right arm dangled a green velvet bag with a gold cord'.

From *circa* 1840, although built-in pockets had returned, some bags continued to be carried, though becoming gradually smaller, resembling a fabric purse or handkerchief sachet and sometimes worn on sashes across the body. Nancy Bradfield (1968, p.153) describes an outfit in the Snowshill Manor Collection, National Trust, of a purple-black satin underdress with matching gauze overdress, and a reticule or handkerchief sachet in silk, embroidered with chenille, ribbon work and petals made from tiny white fish scales; all lined in pink silk, the flap fastening with a tiny pearl button. By the next decade typical shapes included the hexagon or a horseshoe, and many were embellished with floral patterns worked in glass beads. Large-scale patterns that could be executed quickly such as Native American motifs were popular, as were 'Turkish' designs worked in braid, inspired by the Crimean War (1853–6), or 'beetle-wing' spangles. Like the heavy satin and chenille work which was also popular, their density reflected the heavier dress fabrics of the time.

Berlin Woolwork and Art Needlework

Queen Adelaide sat down to work when the King sat down to cards, & was very busy counting the stitches of a Berlin pattern, but talking to the Ladies sitting round the table with her. (Lady Wharncliffe's description of a dinner she attended in 1832 at the Brighton Pavilion: Groves 1966)

The Handbook of Useful and Ornamental Amusements of 1845 was typical of numerous manuals that provided patterns and inspiration for domestic pursuits. Fashion information became even more widely disseminated as women's magazines flourished following the abolition of paper tax in the 1850s. From the 1830s Berlin woolwork dominated home embroidery. The patterns were worked in merino wools from Germany on to canvas, and silks were introduced for texture and bright colour contrasts. Thousands of printed charts were imported into England, each square representing a stitch, and many designs for bags and purses were available, as well as for other small objects such as slippers or watch holders, while more ambitious projects such as pictures and upholstered stools were made on a coarser canvas weave. The finished product was hard wearing and durable. While much of the embroidery was worked simply and methodically, more complex stitches and patterns were often used for bags (plate 30). Small, geometric patterns were popular at first, but soon floral

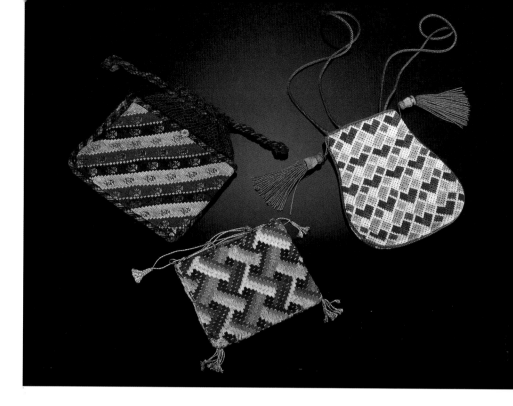

motifs became highly prevalent. These began with an early fineness and delicacy of scale worked against a light background, followed by large-scale and brightly coloured pattern worked against a dark background. From the 1830s Berlin woolwork incorporated beads, resulting in compositions of great variety and colour (plate 31).

By 1866 the *Magazine of Art* (quoted in the *Needleworkers' Dictionary,* 1978) wrote that Berlin woolwork 'has left in its wake vestiges not even now effaced, in the shape of mats and cushions coarsely worked on strong magentas and violent spinach greens ... bell-pulls, carpet slippers, braces, handbags ... and anything which fancy or ingenuity could consider decorating'. It took William Morris (1834–96), with his early embroidery of the 1860s, together with the Art Needlework of the 1870s (when the Royal School of Needlework was founded), to come to the rescue of home embroidery. Soon flowing lines and naturalistic designs became popular. By 1876 it was claimed that: 'The seeds of refined taste sown by the "School of Art Needlework" are already bearing fruit' (Cunnington 1938, p.281).

Plate 30 above Three Berlin woolwork purses. British, 1800s. T.1508–1913; T.102–1926; T.1502–1913

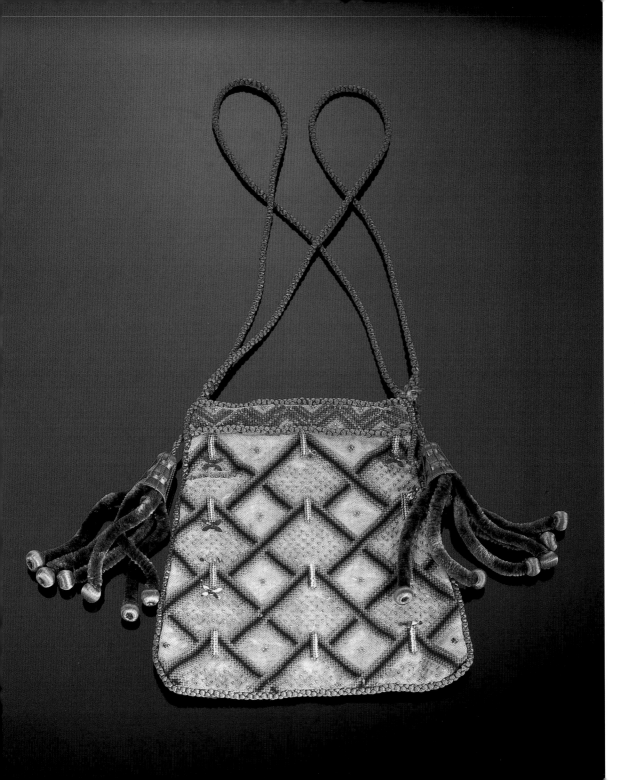

Châtelaines and Nécessaires

Châtelaine translated from the French means 'lady of the castle', or the lady of the house. In keeping with ideals of domesticity derived from earlier times, many women wore numerous small and decorative items such as scissors and pin cushions, keys and note pads, perfume, and often a small purse or bag, suspended by chains from a châtelaine that attached to the waist belt by a large decorated clasp. In the late eighteenth and nineteenth century châtelaines were made of cut-steel, later ivory, pinchbeck and jet for mourning, as well as silver and gold. A typical châtelaine of 1873 of oxidised silver, steel or electroplate would include purse, memo book, scent bottle, pin cushion, thimble, scissors, yard measure and penknife, and was, to a great extent, decorative. Sewing tools were often contained in a 'nécessaire', a small portable case or box made in a diversity of materials. From the 1850s, many nécessaires were made in leather with a small handle, resembling a tiny handbag that hung from two chains, containing a complete set of sewing tools, often beautifully fitted.

From the 1840s, châtelaine bags (described as 'somewhat Scotch and somewhat oriental' by the *Englishwoman's Domestic Magazine* of 1861; Foster 1982, p.49) were increasingly popular, and hung from the waist belt by a cord or hook and chain. By 1856 the fashion for vast skirts stretched over a crinoline rendered any pocket but the most diminutive unsightly. Châtelaine bags were useful for coins and small items. These were made of fabric or leather and usually fastened with a flap; many were made to match the dress. They remained popular for the rest of the nineteenth century (plate 32), their versatility suiting changing styles of dress, in particular the narrow draped skirts of the 1870s. By the end of the century, leather châtelaine bags with flap fronts and applied decorative metal plaques were popular for shopping or travelling, and some came with their own leather belts.

While the work box was used for sewing at home, work-bags continued to be an important domestic branch of the hand-held bag for visiting or travelling. As in the eighteenth century they assumed symbolic virtues, but in the nineteenth century these were associated with homeliness rather than fashionableness. *The Workwoman's Guide* of 1840 (facsimile, Bloomfield 1995, p.v) describes the concerns of the

Plate 31 opposite Berlin woolwork canvas bag with gilt beads and chenille tassels. British, *c.*1830.

T.286–1973

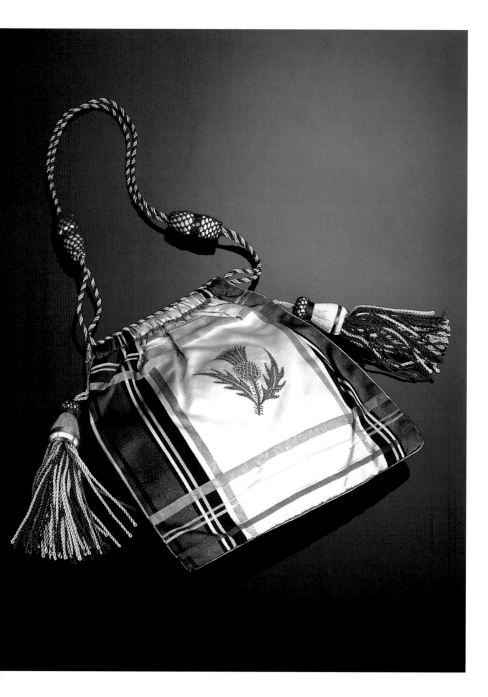

Plate 32 left Silk bag of woven tartan satin with a thistle, trimmed with silk cords and elaborate tassels. British, *c.*1850. Similar to an example in *The Lady's Newspaper* of 1847 (Foster, 1982, p.48). T.397–1910

Plate 33 opposite Group of three purses. Left: purse knitted in coloured silks with steel beads on the point of each leaf-shaped pendant. Possibly Italian, 1800–29. T.1348–1913 Middle: purse knitted in coloured silks with horizontal bands of openwork, silk drawstring and tassels and lined with green silk. British, 1800–49. T.27–1910 Right: knitted purse in the form of a pineapple decorated with white beads, British, 1800s. T.67–1961

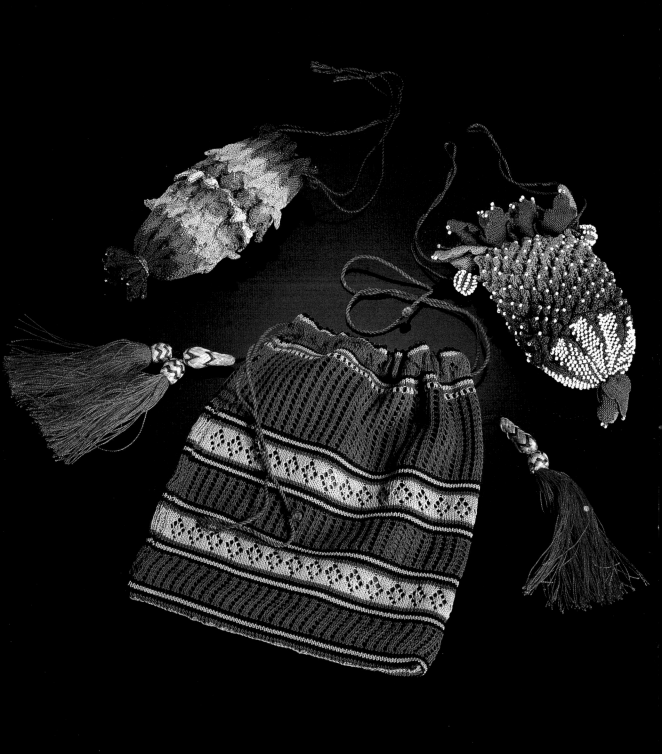

good wife, rather than the fancy work of the privileged: 'The thrifty disposition, the regularity and neatness, the ideas of order and management, inspired by the conscious ability and successful exertion, in one leading branch of good housewifery, cannot be too highly prized or diligently cultivated; for the result is moral.'

Knitted Purses

Many thousands of small purses were knitted, embroidered or crocheted in the nineteenth century (plate 33), intended either for personal use or as a gift or donated to a worthy fundraising cause. Netting was still popular in the early 1800s. In Jane Austen's *Pride and Prejudice* (1813) Mr Bingley observed that fashionable young ladies all could 'paint tables, cover screens and net purses'. Mr Darcy typically replied that young ladies should not be considered accomplished just because they were 'netting a purse, or covering a screen'. Crocheting, incorporating brightly coloured beadwork, was popular in the 1830s, but it was knitting that as a domestic craft reached its peak in the nineteenth century. Knitting thrived as an elegant drawing-room occupation, and much time was devoted to making intricate and delicate items of fancy work without obvious use.

Early nineteenth-century peg-knitted purses and bags were formed in tubes, with a tassel hanging at the base to weight them. Many had simple patterns of stripes and geometric designs such as the Greek key motif. Later these were interspersed with rows of floral motifs. Subsequently knitted purses and bags were usually produced on very fine steel needles, exquisitely knitted in silk and cotton, or even straw, and some incorporate beads (plate 34) that were threaded on to the yarn before knitting. Some present a completely dense surface, with one bead for every stitch worked, enabling complex images to be depicted. These were very popular in the 1830s. Many purses survive from these hours of work, in which the full creative possibilities of fine knitting have been explored with different attractive textures and raised work, beautiful colours and inventive patterns and stitches.

Beadwork was used to record dates and significant events or to bear messages to a loved one. A brown knitted-silk purse with white beads (illustrated in Rutt 1987, p.109) lists the events of the Peninsular

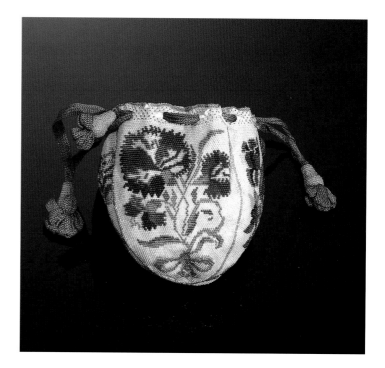

Plate 34 above *Plate 34 above* Small drawstring bag divided into four panels with floral motifs worked in brightly coloured glass beads, knitted to form a dense ground with a bead per stitch. British, early 19th century. T.396–1910

War of 1808–14. Many luxury beaded bags and purses were made in Germany, knitted from yarn pre-strung with beads to form complex floral or landscape patterns; bags with stiffened bases were popular, featuring baskets of flowers, stone urns and oriental figures.

Tiny 'shaggy' purses with raised loops were popular in the 1830s; some of the loops were embellished with steel beads, others were knitted to produce a nubbly texture, shaded and adorned with a single bead at every raised point. Some were attached to tiny frames and closed with a round, mother-of-pearl lid on a steel ring, or had a metal finger-ring (see plate 23). Many seem to have received little wear and tear, indicating that they were perhaps gifts.

The first knitting books appeared between 1835 and 1840, with the emergence of the fancy-wool trade – silky, fine, merino wool in a wide range of shades imported from Germany. One of the first and best-selling printed instruction books was by Mrs Jane Gaugain, *The Lady's Assistant for Executing Useful and Fancy Designs in Knitting,*

Netting and Crochet (1841–6), in three volumes. A knitting pattern from the *Workwoman's Guide* of 1840 (1975, p.273), using colours popular at the time, although bold by later tastes, suggested that a 'reticule bag' could be 'knit in two colours, say violet and green ... this makes a durable handsome bag, and may be knit of even more colours or shades, if preferred'. In Thackeray's novel, *Vanity Fair* (1848), Becky Sharp knits a green purse for Joseph Sedley, for as mentioned before green was the colour of love. Enjoyment of the new palettes allowed by the development of chemical dyes in 1859 could be seen in reinterpretations of traditional patterns such as Fair Isle, in, for example, a knitted purse of brightly coloured silks made in Orkney in the late 1850s.

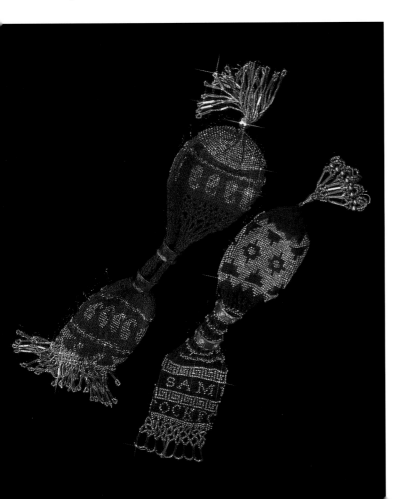

Plate 35 opposite
Beaded stocking purses.
British, 1800s.
T.1395–1913; T.1194–1913

Fig. 13 below Fashionable
walking dress with fur muffs
and attached metal-frame
purses with tassels. *Punch,*
March 1900, p.223. NAL

Wallet or stocking purses were very popular up to the 1860s, and they survive in great numbers, although examples of frame-knitted (machine) purses are rare. Many stocking purses were netted in silk and had steel beads, spangles and paillettes with steel, gilt, silver or gold sliders and tassels; their decoration varied from the minimal to highly patterned. Often they were inscribed and dated, many clearly made as gifts for gentlemen (plate 35).

Filigree metalwork purses of very fine iron wire known as 'Berlin ironwork' were made in tiny coils and formed into patterns in the early nineteenth century; some survive, and the V&A has several examples, although many are fragile and rusted to the point of disintegration. Others were made of fine silver mesh and survive rather better (plate 36). Tiny gold-sovereign purses, which appeared after the introduction of the new coin in 1816, were worked on steel frames with a press-top opening, often in crochet with steel beads. From the middle of the century there were leather purses, followed by plush, reptile skin and fur towards the end of the century. Later, hinged guinea purses of the 1890s, made of silver and with a concertina kid lining, often had a finger ring in their chain handle. Others were made in a thimble shape in the finest silver-chain mesh and had an expandable ring top and hinged round lid with chain and finger ring. Held in the hand with the ring on the finger these would be unseen and quite secure. At the end of the nineteenth century German silver-mesh purses and rigid, hinged purses with a finger ring were imported in great numbers.

Purse Muffs and Dorothy Bags

From the 1860s muffs often contained a small inside pocket in the lining for handkerchief, card case or small change, or had a small tasselled purse attached (fig.13). Astrakhan, Siberian fox and black seal were popular, lined with moiré. By 1882, tiny 'deportment muffs', made of silk or fur, were in vogue and were considered 'a needful accessory to the present mode of walking and carriage, which is trim and rather stiff, with the elbows well held in to the sides'. Quoting from the same source, in 1886 'fur muffs are made extremely small, more like a fur cuff than a real muff, and they generally have a pocket

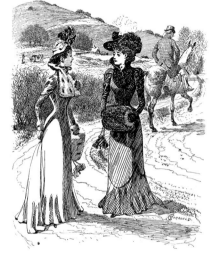

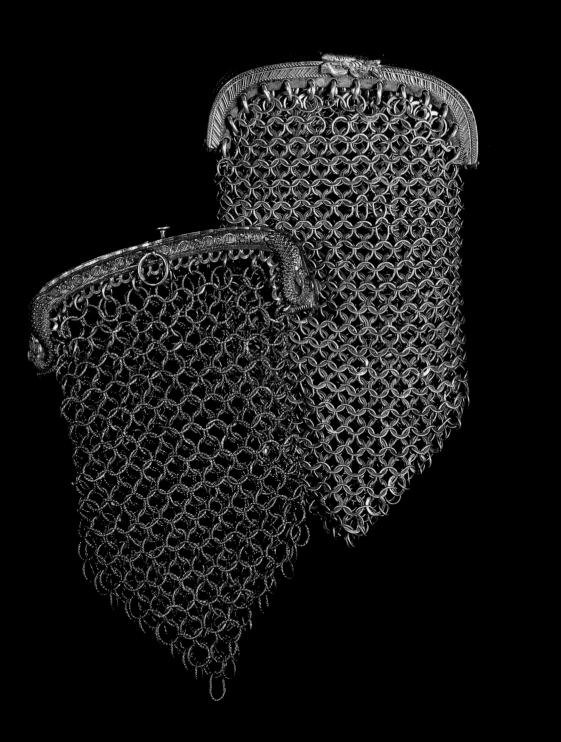

on one side to hold the purse and pocket handkerchief' (Tarrant 1986, p.41). In the same decade there were also large muffs or 'purse muffs', in plush, satin or fur, and their resemblance to bags was marked. Many had a thick handle across the top made of metal or ormolu, which opened up like a bag. In *Victorian Dress in Photographs* (Ginsburg 1982–8, p.84), an unknown Guildford girl wears an astrakhan purse muff made on a straight metal frame with a lift-up opening and rings at the side from which the muff is suspended around the neck on a cord. Others had a short handle and a pocket for the hands at each end.

The charming symmetry of the muff was not provided by the defiantly singular handbag, always held to the side. In the 1880s, the Dorothy bag became popular: it was made of a circle of dress fabric, such as velvet, silk or plush, gathered by a drawstring at the top, leaving fabric for a frill and bows, and named after *Dorothy,* A. J. Munby's play of the 1880s. The Dorcas bag, a variation that had a stiffened base, was also popular. These constituted the last stylistic changes of the fabric reticule of the nineteenth century, soon to be taken over by the much more durable handbag.

Travel Bags

The increase in travel was one of the most significant developments of the nineteenth century. As the first home needlework guides and pattern books that became available from the 1840s indicate, with their instructions for travelling bags, increasing mobility was already becoming a possibility for all classes. *The Workwoman's Guide* (1975) of 1840 provided instructions for making a leather 'carriage case' or 'Porte Folio': 'This is very useful for those ladies who drive about constantly in a town, and who have much shopping, or many calls.' An alternative, for paper, bills, pencil and visiting cards, was made of leather, cloth or stamped paper, laid on millboard, or pieces of tin, to form the sides. In 1857, 'patent railway safety pockets' were advertised (Cunnington 1959, p.461), which cost 1/6; these must have been fairly large, for they were intended to be tied under the skirt and to carry papers and money. Security for travelling now became a prerequisite.

Plate 36 opposite Two small chain purses of hand-linked silver rings, with silver frames. British, 1816–17.
T.260 & T.262–1916

With the development of trains, and the move away from horse-drawn travel, professional luggage makers turned the skills of saddlery into those for train or boat. Luggage styles changed to suit the new medium – for example trunks in the later nineteenth century became flat topped rather than rounded so that they could be stacked. Security became ever more significant, resulting in increasingly sophisticated metal locks and fastenings. Luggage was carried by porters, but the personal essentials for a journey were held in travelling bags or 'carpet' bags (in fact often Berlin-woolwork canvas bags) or the sturdy, leather portmanteau, usually carried by a man (its name deriving from the French word for a bag for carrying a cloak). Mention is often made of the dressing baskets or cases that women carried. These were lighter and for overnight essentials.

In the 1880s, leather bags on a long strap worn across the shoulder became common (fig. 14). It was still a sign of social standing to carry very little. A lady of leisure would carry nothing more than a small bag between the fingers, the rest dealt with by porters or servants. By the late nineteenth century luggage construction had reached its apotheosis with Louis Vuitton's canvas-covered trunks, their interiors fitted with drawers and hanging rails, for epic journeys by rail or boat. Edith Wharton in 'Souls Belated', written at the turn of the century, described one such departure: 'I was sitting in the window, watching for you, when the five o'clock boat left, and who should go on board, bag and baggage, valet and maid, dressing bags and poodle, but Mrs Cope' (Penguin 1995 edition, p.41).

Fig. 14 below Fashion plate for *Mode Illustrée,* April 1880, plate 21. Two women purchase a ticket for a journey by train. One wears an across-the-shoulder bag with flap closing and long strap attached by rings. On a bench is a portmanteau, cloak and parasol. NAL

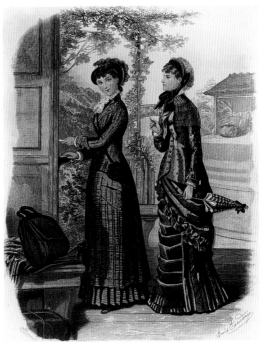

Chapter Six
The Handbag: 1880–1918

Many solid leather bags of a rich brown hue soon surrounded them, in addition to which Mr Dalloway carried a dispatch box, and his wife a dressing-case suggestive of a diamond necklace and bottles with silver tops.
(Virginia Woolf, *The Voyage Out,* 1915: Penguin edition 1970, p.36)

The term 'handbag' first referred to the hand-held luggage bags usually carried by men, but in the last third of the nineteenth century practical and stylistic elements of the leather travelling bag, such as its metal fastenings and compartmentalised interior, ticket pockets and sturdy handle, inspired the new handbag for women, the precursor of the twentieth-century handbag. Echoing luggage styles, commercially manufactured leather, silk or velvet handbags with metal frames and fastenings became available. Framed handbags, made in plush with plush handles (see plate 29, right) or in sealskin in the 1860s and 1870s, and in morocco in the late 1870s, followed. By the 1880s, coloured leathers were popular, in morocco and kidskin (plate 37). The very small leather handbags of the late nineteenth century, while extremely small, still alluded to the details of hand luggage with its pockets, complicated fastenings, locks and tiny keys (plate 38).

As women went out and about more, so handbags became more specific to particular occasions. At the turn of the century the skills of the leather- and metalworkers became more commercial, and fitted bags and cases turned the handbag in some cases into a portable miracle of miniaturisation. Equipping the interior of the handbag with fittings for cosmetics, money, opera glasses, fan and, later, cigarettes was undertaken increasingly by jewellers such as Van Cleef & Arpels and Asprey, as purses and handbags became ever more specialised and sophisticated.

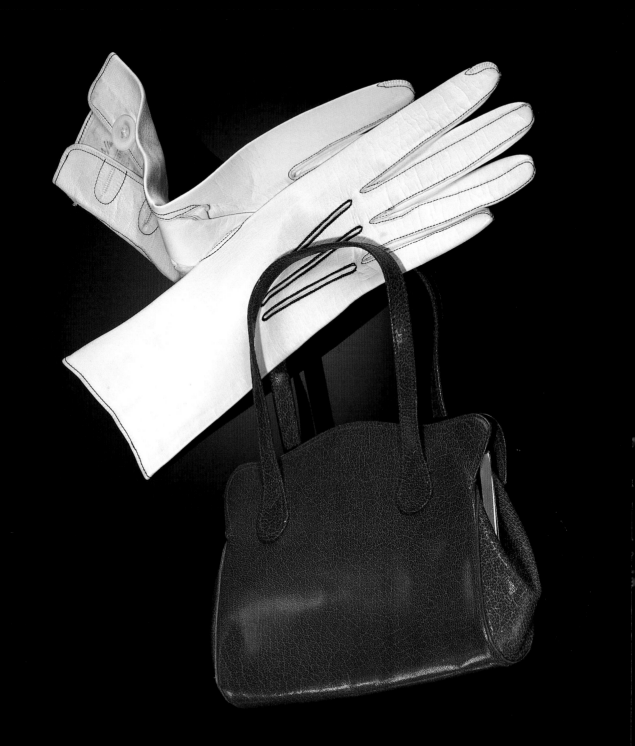

The soft fabric reticules of the nineteenth century had their roots in the domestic work-bag and the textile tradition, and were often carried at home or for evening wear. The leather handbag originated in the saddlery tradition and became an accessory exclusively for use in the public domain, reflecting women's increasing journeys from home into the outside world; their bags accompanied and equipped them for this. In many ways it symbolised women's new-found freedom and independence as women started to travel unaccompanied. Handbags began to provide a refuge from public life; they often incorporated mirrors that could be used to check on one's appearance, apply make-up or discreetly catch a glimpse of another, like portable dressing-tables. Privacy and secrecy became paramount – there was no more showing of female accessories, as with the châtelaine and work box. Although women had been carrying cosmetics in their bags in the form of packets of rouge and face powder since the early nineteenth century, putting on a public face became a dominant theme of the twentieth century. By the early 1900s, the handbag was essential to a new breed of working, travelling women. Unlike men with their numerous and capacious pockets, women have more or less since that time kept one hand firmly on their handbag.

1900–1907

The first few years of the new century saw, for the lady of leisure, a continuation of the fashionable preoccupations of the last. Feminine, ornate clothes in pastel shades appeared soft and lacy but were underpinned by rigid corseting, rendering women shapely but inflexible. Small silver or gold chain purses were popular, drawstring or on frames, and were held by chain and finger-ring, fixed at the waist or pinned to the bodice, or hung like a necklace on long chains and tucked into the belt: 'equally attractive were purses of silver "fish scales" with big substantial silver tops, not to speak of a variety of new gold purses fringed with gold balls. Anything prettier I can hardly imagine' (*Tatler*, 19 November 1902, p.318).

Those contained in handbags included morocco-leather purse and card cases with silver corners, with folders for the newly invented pound note (which replaced the gold sovereign in 1914). For the

Plate 37 opposite Glacé-grained kid leather bag with a metal hinged frame with twist fastening. British, 1890s. The bag is made from a single piece of leather with a gusset inserted at each end. The top is scalloped so that the frame is concealed, and a side pocket is formed either side of the centre pouch. Two handles are machine stitched to each side.

T.216–1983

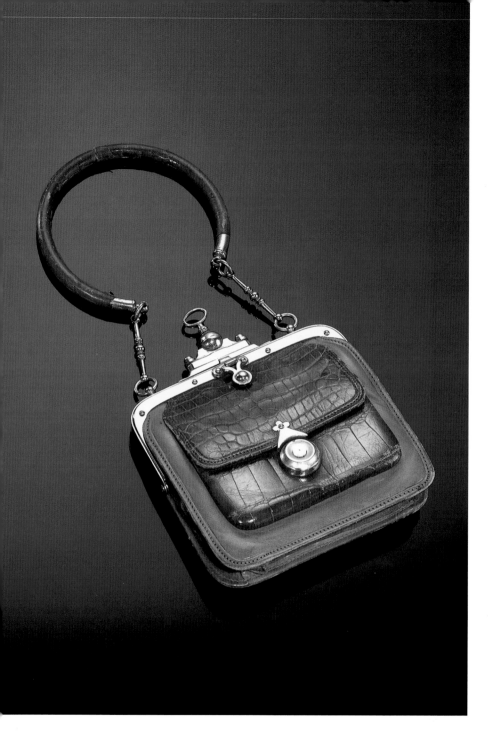

Plate 38 left Brown leather handbag with an external purse of crocodile skin, lined with kid. British *c.*1889. With chrome clasp and fittings, original key, and metal leather-covered handle. The donor was for many years in charge of the handbag department at Selfridges.
T.61–1956

Plate 39 opposite Brown leather crocodile effect bag with chrome metal mounts, fastening with a leather strap and locking button with leather handles. Possibly French, *c.*1900. The bag contains an imitation ivory note tablet and a purse.
T.203&A–1975. Grey doeskin glove. French, *c.*1900.
T.1A–1968

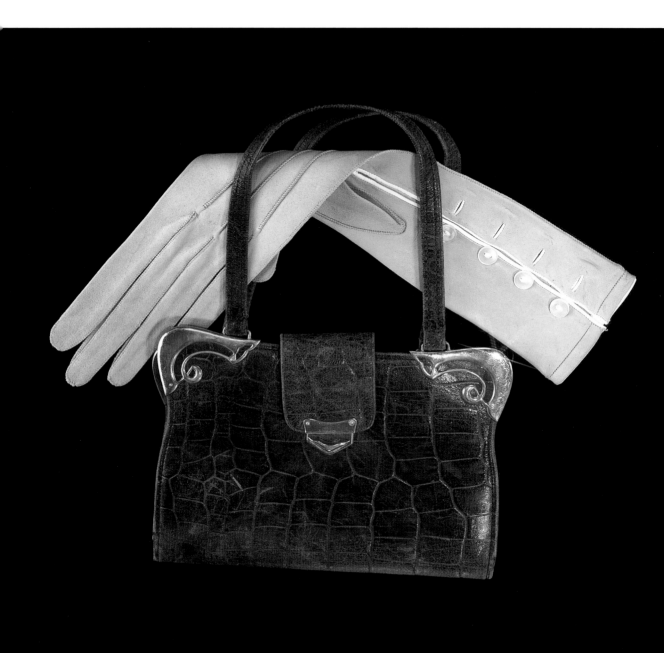

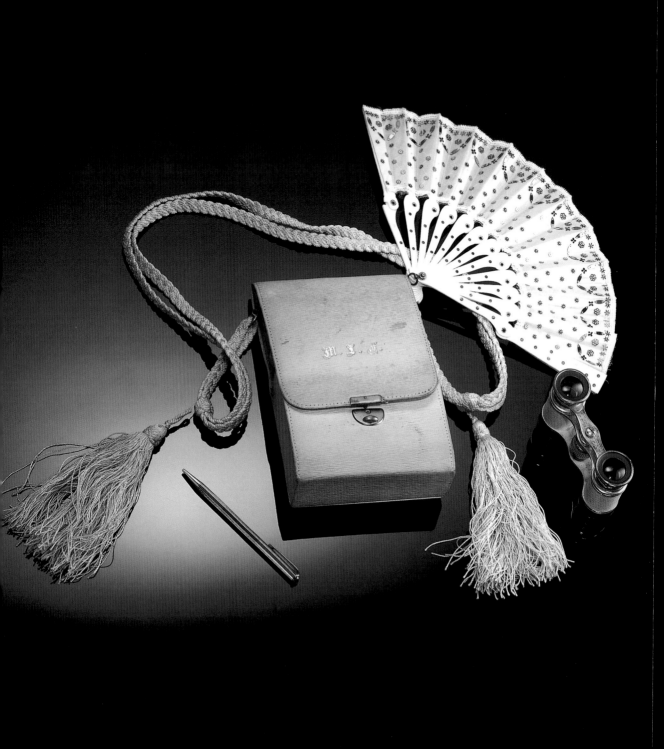

adventurous, there were leather 'cycling' belts with an attached purse.

Typical for leisured day wear were smart tailor-made suits of skirt and long jacket worn with large hats and accompanied by envelope 'Boulevard' bags or tiny leather handbags with shaped handles, trim and neat, decorated with silver corners (plate 39). For the drawing-room there were lace-insertion and sequinned-net Dorothy bags worn with matching robes; circular bags of crochet lace over white moire, the pattern of the lace worked out in pearls; bags studded with opals or with lines of sequins running down them; and charming pompadour confections in flowered and striped silks. Beadwork and embroidery remained popular, and hand-beaded steel châtelaine bags were mentioned in the *Tatler* in December 1901 (p.505). Magazines of the day describe bags for every occasion, from fitted leather bags with telescopic opera glasses and folding fan (plate 40) to drawstring theatre bags with a mirror set into the base. There were leather 'shopping' bags and even briefcase bags, for many more women were entering the professional work force and supported women's suffrage.

From 1907 an elongated look began to replace the sinuous s-curve of the 1900s. This was reminiscent of fashions of the 1800s and, in acknowledgement, referred to at the time as the Directoire style. As in the previous *fin-de-siècle,* handbags multiplied. In London, Liberty's in Regent Street began to sell 'Oriental' bags, reflecting the interest in chinoiserie, and Paul Poiret's designs, inspired by the colours and exoticism of the Ballet Russes, were highly influential. Curved jewelled frames held on long tasselled cords, embroidered fabric bags gathered at the base to a large tassel that nearly swept the floor and beaded bags with Chinese and Japanese scenes completed the obsession with Orientalism.

A vogue for large bags and briefcases, carried or worn across the shoulder with hobble skirts and large hats, was lampooned mercilessly by *Punch* (1910): 'Good gracious, my dear girl, do you think I should put anything in this bag? It's as much as I can carry empty!' By 1913, bag designs became calmer as war approached: for day, grey antelope and crocodile with external pockets and fitted interior with puff; for evening, black-and-white striped satin, black velvet and ermine, velvet and embroidered satin, and a bevelled mirror forming the base.

Plate 40 opposite
Monogrammed (M.L.F.) leather opera bag with a plaited silk handle with matching tassels. French, *c.*1910. By Lemiere. Flap fastening has a brass lever catch. Contains a change purse, mirror, bone note card, pencil, swansdown powder puff, telescopic opera glasses, and white organdie folding fan with gilt spangles. T.219–F–1965

1914–18

The upkeep of the high-maintenance, fashionable wardrobe of the 1900s had depended on an army of domestics and ladies' maids. With the advent of the First World War (1914–18) the social structure of society changed, as described in Sonia Keppel's *Edwardian Daughter* (1958):

One of the facts of war that had most impressed me had been Mamma's ability suddenly to do without Miss Draper, and to go off to Etaples with only a small suitcase as her luggage. Now, I recalled the daily services that Miss Draper had always done for Mamma: drawing her bath and scenting it with rose-geranium bath salts; setting out her underclothes under their lace cover; kneeling on the floor to put on Mamma's stockings, lacing Mamma into her stays (as though she were reining in a runaway horse); doing her hair; pinning her veil onto her hat; buttoning up her gloves; putting her powder and cigarettes and money into her bag. And, behind the scenes, washing, ironing, mending. It had quite worried me to think of Mamma bereft of all this help.

Bag fashions soon reflected the nation's preoccupations, and dark velvet or silk with white cord decoration matched military-influenced frogging on the cuffs and lapels of jackets. Black moiré-silk vanity bags were serious and unadorned, on straight or curved frames with loop handles and a tassel at the base. These were fitted with a manicure case, pencil, button hook and nail file, for as the *Tatler* of December 1914 said: 'Now that the war has so drastically reduced our incomes a useful gift is more than ever welcome.' For day, morocco, crocodile or seal was popular, with fitted interiors and 'captive' purses on a chain. As skirts became shorter and flared this was reflected by a move away from the Dorothy bag with its long drawstrings to plumper shapes (plate 41).

Perhaps with a sense that the end of the war was in sight, fur became popular. Erté designed an extremely luxurious ermine wrap with pockets, shown with a black-and-white Dorothy bag, with a ruff falling in tasselled handkerchief points; it was followed in 1918 by a bag with ermine tail fringe and handles, 'so very wide that they may become a stole when one so desires' (Erté design from October 1918, illustrated in Blum 1976), and, even more strangely, an ermine and woven-silk knitting bag, with needles of carved ivory. Fur bags soon appeared in magazines such as the *Queen,* which in December 1919 featured bags made of bands of skunk and gold lace on white satin with an ivory clasp and seal and ermine mounted on to dark tortoise-shell, claiming that: 'Bags can match the fur of your coat, and they can easily be made with bits of fur left over from a collar or renovated coat.' Metal brocade bags on frames of ivory carved into elephants or Chinese figures and dance bags of silver or gold tissue with metal lace and a mirror base were also popular.

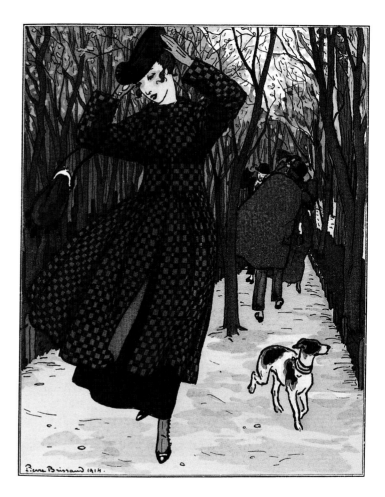

Plate 41 right Fashion plate from *Gazette du Bon Ton,* April 1914, showing spring fashions. Four months before the outbreak of War, skirts have already begun to rise and become fuller, and the curved frame and full body of the handbag reflect this.

Chapter Seven

Dance Bags, Clutches and 'Make-do-and-Mend': 1918–1945

There are gentlemen jockeys, lady air-pilots, titled crooks … A decade has changed the world. (British *Vogue,* January, 1924)

The many activities that became accessible to women after the war demanded accessories. As different methods of travel became widely available, so luggage manufacturers responded to these new needs, as reported in the *Queen* (29 November 1919, p.719):

A fitted handbag is one of the necessities of life for a motorist, and even if it were not there would be every reason for congratulating oneself on becoming the possessor of that gem of a lady's motor bag in morocco leather of a deep, full violet lined with old gold watered silk, and containing the completest set of engine turned silver gilt toilet requisites that the heart of the traveller by motor-car could desire.

Clothes in the early 1920s were liberating. Gone were long, constricting layers and rigid corseting. Fewer items were worn, and the effect was lighter, emphasising youth rather than maturity. Hemlines varied from long and narrow to crinoline shaped or fell in handkerchief points to the floor. The British fashion magazine *Femina* of August 1920 noted that (p.14): 'As there are hours in the day, so there are bags, veritable artistic bibelots both in form and colour.' Bags did not match an outfit, they contributed towards the general decorative effect. Novelty bags of 1921 included doll-bags. 'The matron who would be correct may carry a doll dressed exactly like herself. The skirt of mauve and white taffeta embroidered in orange is an efficient hand-bag' (Blum 1976). Floral purse-bags could be attached to the corsage and resembled a bunch of flowers; there were butterfly-shaped bags and ostrich-feather purses with cords and tassels, and

Plate 42 opposite Green-felt handbag with applied bands of black and gold leather and an appliqué design of birds in an Egyptian style. British or French *c*.1924. The clasp is of brass with lapis lazuli coloured trimming and the handle of gold wire cord. The bag is lined with yellow satin and has two pockets and a mirror and powder wallet.
T.236&A–1972

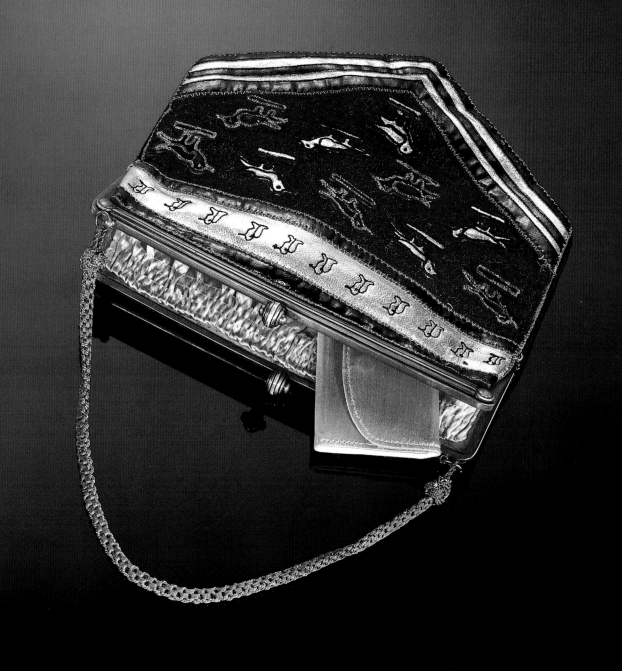

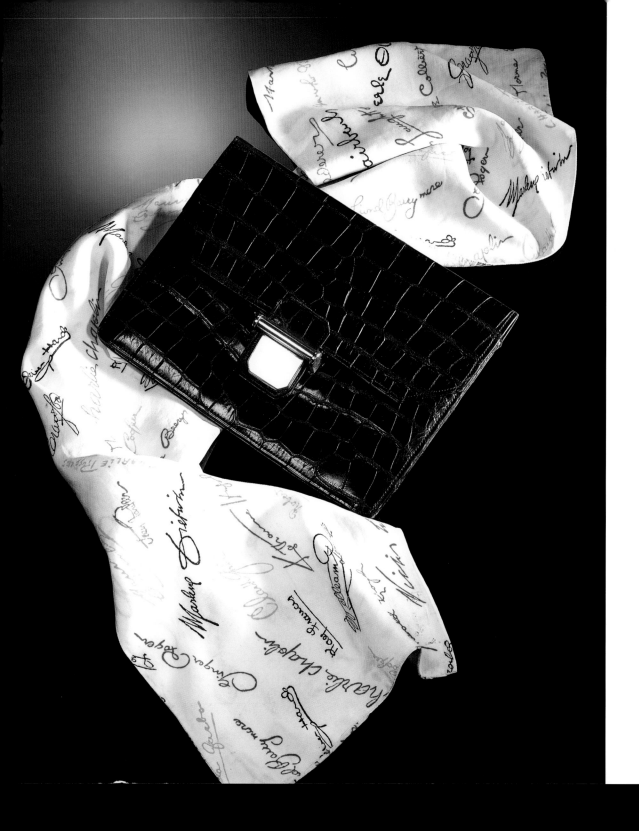

glove purses of embroidered white suede, with long tasselled exten-sion from the wrist in which to tuck a handkerchief. Most extra-ordinary was Dunhill's 'Lytup' handbag of 1922, which lit up when opened – 'invaluable in a taxi or wherever the lights are dim' (*Tatler*, 31 May 1922, p.viii) – while the *Sketch* of 12 December 1928 featured a bag in the shape of a motor car from Finnigans, a leading bag manufacturer, with a door that opened to reveal a mirror.

For the first half of the twenties, framed handbags remained pop-ular, deep and curved, with a full, gathered fabric pouch, often heavily beaded or, for day, in plain taffeta. Ornate frames carved from ivory with Chinese embroidery were as fashionable as they had been in the 1910s, but 'simuli' ivory, or early plastic, was a less costly alternative. Straight frames with a chain handle were also popular, and comple-mented geometric patterns in leather patchwork or embroidery. The discovery in 1922 of King Tutankhamun's tomb in Egypt inspired a wealth of Egyptomania in the applied arts (plate 42), from fabrics to jewellery and make-up, although these preoccupations pre-dated Carter's discovery. In *Bliss and Other Stories*, 'The Escape', a short story written in 1920 about the breakdown of a couple's relationship while abroad, Katherine Mansfield described a handbag and its contents with emotive power:

The little bag, with its shiny, silvery jaws open, lay on her lap. He could see her powder-puff, her rouge stick, a bundle of letters, a phial of tiny black pills like seeds, a broken cigarette, a mirror, white ivory tablets with lists on them that had been heavily scored through. He thought: 'In Egypt she would have been buried with these things.'

For the very smart, in 1924–5 issue seven of *Gazette du Bon Ton* showed a lizard-skin bag with over-arm handle by Hermès, similar to one in the V&A (plate 43), but between 1925 and 1930 the envelope-shaped 'pochettes' began to dominate, some with residual handles at top or back, through which the fingers could slip, others with a frame but no handle, to tuck under the arm, in 1926 becoming very large. Some closed with an envelope flap with an asymmetrically placed metal catch, while the flap in others covered the whole side, provid-ing an uninterrupted expanse for the latest styles in Art Deco, dazzling

Plate 43 opposite Black crocodile rectangular handbag with flap fastening. French, *c*.1931. By Hermès. The silver clasp is on a cylindrical hinge that passes through a silver-mounted slit in a tongue attached to the bag flap. The clasp is hallmarked and incised 'Hermès'. On the reverse is a finger strap. The bag is lined with grey leather and has pockets. It is thought to be one of Hermès' early designs. Silk scarf printed with signatures of film stars. Late 1930s. T.225–1969: T.286–1978

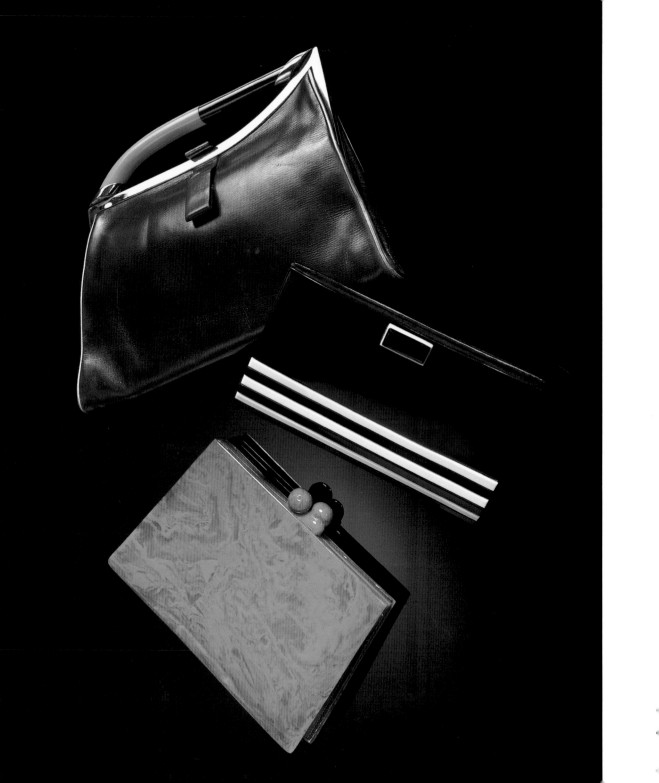

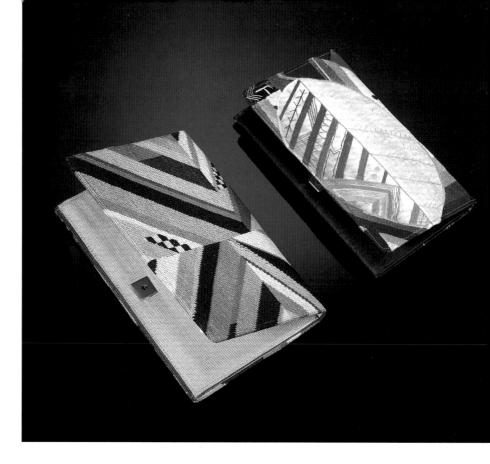

Plate 44 opposite Group of three pochettes. Top: black calf-leather pochette with a chrome frame and curved yellow and green plastic handle, with blue moiré lining with central change purse and powder wallet. British, *c.*1926. T.235&A –1972 Middle: small pochette striped in black lacquer and ivory plastic, silk lined. French, *c.*1925. T.237&A–1982 Bottom: green-silk pochette of rectangular shape with green-plastic sides and frame, marbled in bright green and semi-translucent emerald shades. French, *c.*1925. The frame has two spherical knobs that lock to form the clasp. The green watered-silk lining has a mirror pocket. Circ.273–1971

Plate 45 right Two embroidered bags. Austrian, *c.*1925. By Hilde Wagner-Ascher. In the early 1920s Hilde Wagner-Ascher studied under Josef Hoffmann in Vienna. T.284–1987; T.285–1987

geometric patterns and sunbursts, stylised figures and jazz motifs. While leather, shagreen and suede were common, pochettes were the perfect vehicle for early plastics such as Bakelite, which was formed in sheets. Plastics flourished; having originally been a substitute for expensive materials such as ivory and tortoiseshell, they were lightweight and easy to form into shapes, ideal for mass production (plate 44).

The 1925 Exhibition of Decorative Arts in Paris defined innovative designs and modern motifs, a style in which art and industry merged (plate 45). These bold new styles could be applied to goods on a mass scale and were typified by a decisive geometry and an element of romantic figuration, depicting the speed of transport or dancing figures. Art Deco had a great influence on jewellery design, and companies such as Tiffany, Boucheron and Cartier made many small, expensive accessories that were related to the handbag, such as tiny vanity and cigarette cases. Many vanity cases took the form of a small cylinder, with chain and finger-ring, and attached lipstick cases, while others concealed the lipstick in a large silk tassel (plate 46). Van Cleef & Arpels was well known for their minaudière, a large, solid, flat metal purse that was said to be inspired by American socialite Florence Jay Gould, who used a cigarette tin for a purse. This held cigarettes, make-up and money in its compartmentalised interior and was often lavishly jewelled. Designs of the 1920s typically featured black enamel and diamanté (plate 47), while others were embellished with real gems such as Cartier's evening bags, some in enamelled gold and diamonds with Pharaonic motifs. Another Cartier purse, its frame set with diamonds, emeralds, rubies and sapphires, was beaded all

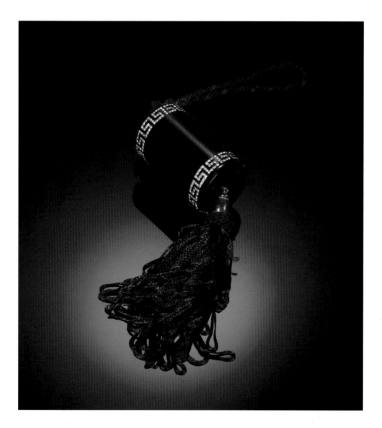

Plate 46 left Cylindrical 'dance' purse made of black plastic and diamanté. British, late 1920s. By J.A.C. Hinged, it opens to reveal a lipstick. Held with a black silk cord, it has a large black silk tassel.
T.30&A–1981

Plate 47 opposite Evening purse of fine metal mesh with a silver frame, and black and white enamelled clasp and pearl drop detail held by a leather-lined black wrist strap. French, *c.*1925.
Circ.245–1971

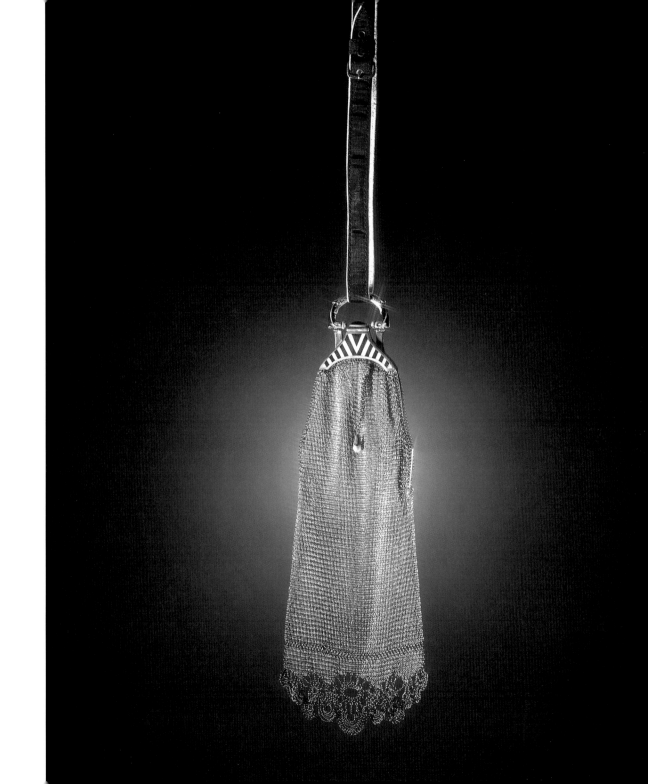

over, fringed with cultured pearls and held by a silk cord with jewelled beads. Yet others had a watch set into the frame or forming the
clasp, with geometric and stylised floral motifs identifying them
closely with this uniquely rich and exuberant period.

As the 1920s progressed, skirts grew shorter and the flapper was
born, with her bobbed hair, smoking and drinking cocktails from
America. Fringed beaded handbags matched beaded evening dresses,
which, loosely cut and simply styled, with their weight emphasised
every movement (plate 48). Dance craze followed dance craze, from
the Charleston to the Black Bottom, which had taken over from the
foxtrot and the waltz, and when Josephine Baker and La Revue Nègre
came to Paris the effect was electrifying. A result of a new cosmopolitanism, exotic designs from Africa, Egypt, Morocco and the Far
East were absorbed into popular art and fashion. Sybil Pendlebury, in
British *Vogue* (November 1925, p.118), describes how: 'A charming
ensemble is composed of a hat and a handbag made from a piece of
oriental embroidery with a sphinx and palm-tree design in rich
colours'. By the end of the twenties, bags had become wider than they
were deep. Magnificent mounts in marcasite complemented black-
suede, diamanté pochettes with jazz designs in brilliants. Petit-point
bags at Liberty's in London, each bag taking four months to make,
signalled a new romanticism.

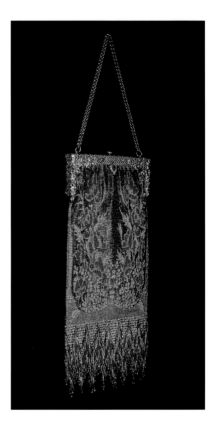

The 1930s

By the exercise of intelligence we can force the machine into the service of
beauty. (C. A. Glasgold, *Design in America,* 1930)

The freedoms gained for women in the 1920s with the gamine look of
shorter skirts and cropped hair seemed to be threatened when 1930s'
fashions appeared to be returning to a long skirted, womanly helpless-
ness. Perhaps due to this concern, long skirts became popular just for
evening wear, while daytime fashions remained at mid-calf (fig. 15).
This compromise gave women the best of both worlds, for the tailored
look of day was offset by a very feminine, svelte look for the evening.
The ideal woman became something of a hybrid, in smart tailor-mades
during the day, heavily made-up and clad in backless satin evening

Plate 48 opposite Beaded and fringed bag with a pattern of red poppies on a dark-blue background and a shaped border of gold beads. French, *c.*1920–30. The frame is gilt metal in the form of trelliswork with roses and has a round button fastening and double chain handle. It is lined with pink silk. The bag is French and was made by Madame Belville in her studio in Paris; she had a small factory where the beads were specially made. T.162–1961

Fig. 15 below Fashion plate from *Vogue Pattern Book,* June-July 1927, p.33. Shows knee-length summer outfits with dropped waist and clutch bag, typical of the late 1920s. NAL

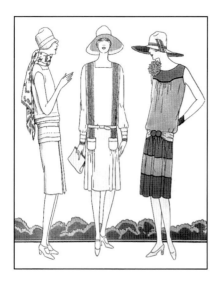

gowns by night, images influenced by Hollywood films. Handbags were smoother and plainer, in keeping with the dominant American aesthetic of streamlining, an interpretation of Art Deco that excluded the romantic figuration of European Art Deco. Leaving only the abstract, uncluttered and aerodynamic, this aesthetic celebrated the new industrial materials, chrome, Vitrolite glass, and plastics, with their sleek and shiny qualities.

These qualities were echoed in fashion by bias-cut, artificial-silk underwear, satin and crêpe dresses cut on the cross to hug the figure, with zips for a closer fit. Zips were also used for handbags. The 'Kashandy' brand featured an advertisement in the July 1933 issue of *Vogue* for bags with 'a zip fastener purse in the handle – a woman must have thought of that!' Evening bags were glamorous and smaller than day bags, smooth and tactile in sequins and beads. There was a new self-consciousness about appearances, an artificiality, reinforced by cosmetics, all of which had an impact on handbag design. Co-ordination became a key word, and, for day, large, smart, capable and capacious handbags in expensive leathers, with chrome and brass fittings, closed with a satisfying clunk. Fully fitted and heavy, the grown-up handbag had finally arrived. Fashion magazines featured articles with titles such as 'Lessons in Chic', and books were full of good advice about co-ordinating the wardrobe. In a Women's Institute publication, *'Harmony in Dress' circa* 1930, p.10, the reader was advised to: 'Carry your purse as though you are proud of it, and it has a decorative as well as utilitarian function. Have it a size to be in harmony with your size, of a colour and texture appropriate for your costume, and matching your shoes, or your gloves, or both.' The smart Hellstern bag, illustrated on the front of this book's jacket, has matching shoes and forms part of a complete ensemble.

The clutch, as the pochette was now called, was either handle-less or had a residual handle and was typically plain and smoothly con-toured. Vanity cases, produced by cosmetic companies such as Elizabeth Arden (plate 49), began to appear for travel and were fully fitted. A new cosmopolitanism associated with air travel and the cruise liner influenced handbag design, sometimes literally, just as the car had inspired a motor-car shape earlier: 'the calf bag in an engaging

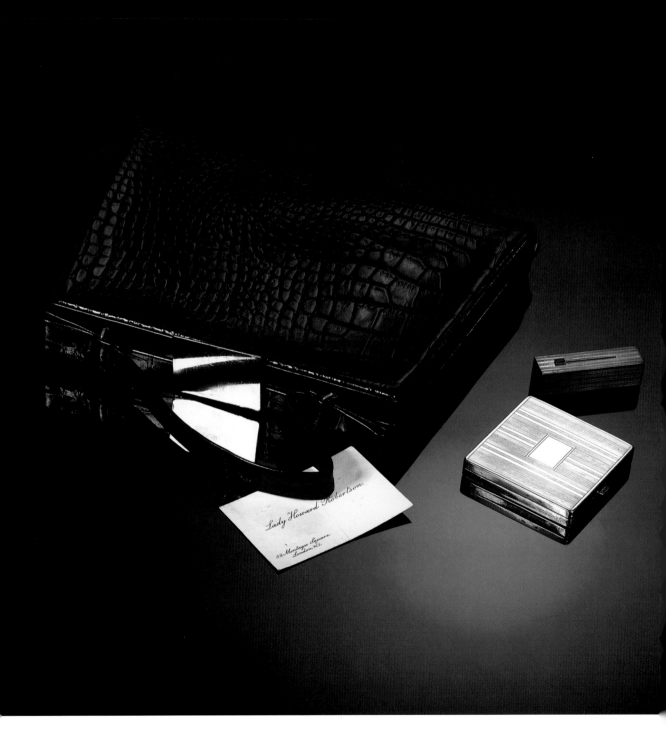

new boat shape has a tuck-in flap and pockets inside and out' (British *Vogue,* 26 June 1935, p.64). The Tassenmuseum, in the Netherlands, has a bag shaped like an ocean liner, complete with chrome funnels and named after the SS *Normandie,* and British *Vogue* in its 26 June 1935 issue described how: 'The new giant liners, the *Queen Mary* and the SS *Normandie,* have set everyone thinking in superlatives. So for the largest ships and the longest decks be ready with the smartest travel coat you could choose … and [for example] a Germaine Guérin crocodile bag.'

By 1935, although war was not to begin for another four years, a consciousness of military detailing appeared with squarer shoulders, skirts a little briefer and Schiaparelli's braiding on a coat with epaulettes. 'You know that the couture has executed a military manoeuvre, and that your day clothes will be martial in spirit,' wrote British *Vogue* in its 2 October issue. Black was in favour, it continued: 'Black uniforms. A bit of braid, an edge of soutache', but this, it elaborated, gave accessories even more importance: 'For town, sulphur suede gloves and matching bag from Molyneux … A cherry red velvet minaudière for my black dinner dress'. Most importantly, straps began to come back, and the pochette was designated more of an evening bag. Bags became large and pouched, on straight frames and with short over-arm handles, as *Vogue* confirmed once more in October 1935:

And bags. They're still big and pouchy. Box calf for your least formal one. With a strap – which you'll find comfortable after all the months you've gripped your purse under your arm. Perhaps this has something to do with army regulations too; knapsack bags when you're at ease and dangle them by the handle [sic]. We've already seen several smart women swinging them that way. A small point but it looks new. Try it.

By now, handbags were being designed by the top fashion designers, in acknowledgement of their significance as they incorporated accessories into their total look. In the pages of *Vogue* there were bags by Schiaparelli, Maggy Rouff, Phillipe Model and Paquin, while jewellers such as Asprey as well as shops such as Jaeger, Harrods, Harvey Nichols and Fortnum & Mason sold bags. Schiaparelli's Surrealist wit extended to her handbag designs: the brown suede bag 'that really

Plate 49 opposite Handbag of black crocodile leather with a gilt clasp and single handle. USA, 1939. By Elizabeth Arden. Lined in black satin, it has a mirror and square gilt powder compact and gilt lipstick. The inside of the bag is stamped 'Elizabeth Arden Patent'. It was given by Elizabeth Arden to the donor when visiting the USA in 1939 for the World's Fair.
T.279-B-1975

looks like a snail' (British *Vogue,* 9 June 1937), her postman shoulder bags, her creations in Rhodophane (an early clear plastic) and her bag for Summer 1938: 'Schiaparelli strips the trees of their leaves and sews them, in black suede, all over a football evening bag' (British *Vogue,* 6 July 1938, p.50).

By the end of the decade, the clutch was giving way to large sensible bags on double handles, gathered soft-pouch leather bags with bangle handles and zip fastening, contrasting saddle stitching and tortoise-shell frames. Mainbocher presented a wicker lunch-basket – 'meant not to carry your lunch, but all your valuables' (British *Vogue,* 5 April 1939). And, just before war broke out, Balenciaga presented an outfit in heavy slipper satin with a tiny lime-green bolero, bodice and reticule (fixed at waist) and a long, black, circular skirt, like a requiem for the 1930s.

The 1940s

Gas masks are absolutely universal and perceive that my own cardboard, slung on string, is quite *démodé* and must be supplied with more decorative case. Great variety of colour and material evidently obtainable, from white waterproof to gay red and blue checks. (E. M. Delafield, *The Provincial Lady in Wartime,* 1940)

The war saw the smooth contours of 1930s' fashions change to a more defensive look with square shoulders, short skirts and fitted waists. As women embraced the new austerity measures and fashions slowed down, so accessories, difficult as they were to get hold of, became important as a way of personalising wartime fashions. Bags became larger, more squared-off and more practical, for as British *Vogue* in its May 1943 issue (p.29) decided: 'Big bags are best; they suit our mood for being self-sufficient.'

As supplies became directed towards the war effort, metal frames and zips, mirrors and leather became scarce. In a wartime issue of the American Sears catalogue, it was noted that 'zippers and closures in handbags were made before government restrictions on the use of materials'. Handbag manufacturers looked to other materials, such as wood or plastic, for frames and catches, and employed new synthetics

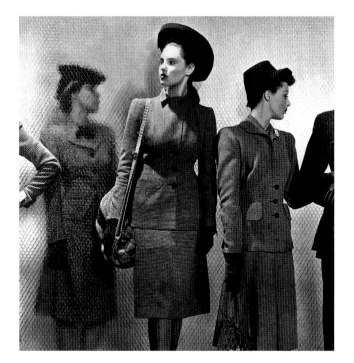

Fig. 16 above Photograph of Utility clothes, designed by the London Couture for the Board of Trade, 1942. *Vogue,* October 1942, p.28. Shows shoulder bag, possibly crocheted in a geometric coloured pattern, and hand-held open string shopping bag. While conforming to the philosophy of 'make do and mend' the inexpensive materials and home-made image of the two bags sit strangely next to the Board of Trade's economically cut but stylishly tailored suits.
PP–1–A

such as curled rayon pile, which resembled black Persian lamb. Wealthier women had their expensive existing handbags remodelled, and 'Make-do-and-Mend' inspired an epidemic of creative home needlework.

Inventive fastenings were employed with buttons and loops or lift-up catches, or abandoned entirely as the drawstring bag reappeared, often home made, but even inspiring major designers. In an article 'Reticules Return', in *Vogue,* March 1940, gold mesh, fringing and tassels are utilised by Balenciaga, satin ruching, braid and draped satin by Paquin. Antique shops were scoured for old frames and beaded purses, which it was suggested could be worn at the waist. Patterns for chunky, crocheted handbags appeared, to be over-sewn to new plastic or old metal frames. Bracelet handles or gathered pouch bags, with wide fabric wrist loops (a fashion that continued after the war), and drawstring collarbox bags with rigid circular bases were featured for evening wear. In 'Bags out of Bits', in *Vogue,* January 1942, three versions of the same pattern are shown: 'Bags, exempt from rationing but priced above rubies, will soon be every woman's desire. Here is a new use for cherished pieces of satin, scraps of heavy material or fur fabric which must now be put into currency.'

For day, there were simple envelope shapes in coloured hessian, knotted string, webbing, gingham and felt with contrasting topstitching, while commercial manufacturers made smart handbags from woollen broadcloth and tweed, as a substitute for leathers, which, always expensive, became unaffordable for most. Styles were generally large, flat and plain, square rather than rectangular.

The shoulder bag (fig. 16) so associated with wartime fashions had first appeared in the late 1930s in designs by Elsa Schiaparelli. In 1940 it was shown with a long strap, small tilted hat and coat with military side buttoning, but, perhaps because of its associations with Forces styles and the gas-mask bag, was far out featured by other types of bags in British *Vogue,* despite being widely popular and practical. Special shoulder bags to carry the gas mask, compulsory in Britain, were made to match an outfit, or commercially in leather by companies such as H. Wald & Co. Again gas-mask bags featured little in the top magazines. After the War, the shoulder bag was relegated to country and travel features, until its revival in the 1970s.

By 1945, enormous, flat envelope bags and solid leather shoulder bags were found, with waist bags on matching belts. By the late forties, commercially manufactured boxy handbags were popular, in all shapes (plate 50). Schiaparelli made bags with compartments and concertinaed bags; there were bags with an external pocket for cigarettes, and all were deeper rather than wide. Improvements in plastics during the war and synthetics such as washable white peccary, vinylite and koroseal benefited fashion, while Vynide and imitation patent were used to satisfy the demands of the consumer, for, as *Vogue,* commented: 'better a good plastic than a poor leather' (Foster 1982, p.77).

By 1948 it was 'accessories unlimited – no more excuses for "making do"' (*Vogue,* October 1948). Styles were still large and structured or smaller, pouched and casual, to hang at the wrist. The materials were unornamented, but the shapes brisk against tweeds, or bright, as in red-and-white striped calf for afternoon in 1949, while brocade clutches on jewelled frames were popular for evening.

Restrictions did not cease immediately after the war, and, despite the introduction of Christian Dior's New Look in 1947, which brought the small clutch straight back into fashion, many women could not afford the latest fashions, and there were a number of protests and demonstrations. The new style, with its voluminous, long skirts and tiny waist was the antithesis of military styles, and it heralded a decade of femininity.

Plate 50 opposite Black-plastic handbag with a wrist strap, gilt frame and clasp. British, *c.*1945-7. T.821–1974

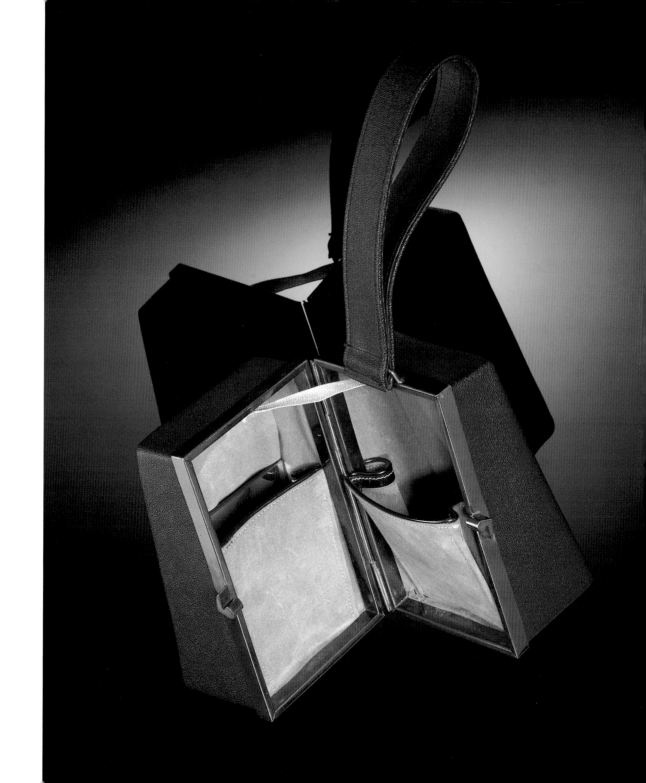

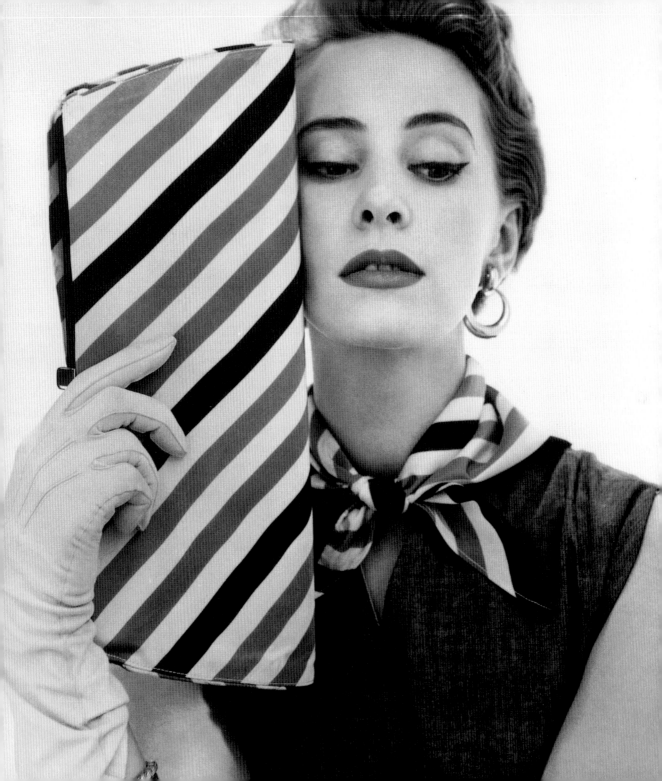

Chapter Eight

The New Look, Shoulder Bags and Designer Handbags

A good handbag is something one can afford to be snobbish about; it is so very much a sign of good grooming. A real telltale, open or shut. (Dora Shackell, *Accent on Accessories,* 1957)

The 1950s were a decade when the importance of order in the home and order in one's appearance was a priority; as Europe set about rebuilding itself, suburbs spread, and fashions became more accessible to an increasingly affluent society. Many of the technological developments of the war effort were redirected to industry, and fashion, as a vital economic force, benefited. Women's fashions were divided between the full skirts and nipped-in waists of the New Look; the slim, vertical look espoused by Jacques Fath in 1953, and, in the late fifties, the Princess line. The importance of accessorising and colour co-ordinating was demonstrated by the number of publications and magazine features on the subject. Stores such as Hattie Carnegie in New York provided a 'hat-to-hem' service and had special pocket-book departments where handbags were made to order. Matching ensemble to accessories was very fashionable (fig. 17), and companies such as Rayne provided shoes and bags in any colour (plate 51).

Companies and shops began to specialise in selling handbags. There was Jane Shilton, H. Wald & Co. (see frontispiece), Fior (see plate 52) and Finnigans in London, Roger Model in Paris and, in America, Mark Cross (famous in Hitchcock's film of 1954, *Rear Window,* for the box bag in which Grace Kelly puts her negligée and slippers). Individual handbag designs began to have a fashionable and cultural significance: Chanel's '2.55' quilted bag with chain handle, named for the date on which it emerged; Louis Vuitton's Noé, a bucket bag originally made for champagne and the company's

Fig. 17 opposite Photograph by John French of a printed-rayon poult handbag and necktie by Madame Crystal, modelled by Barbara Miura, featured in *Harper's Bazaar,* May 1953.

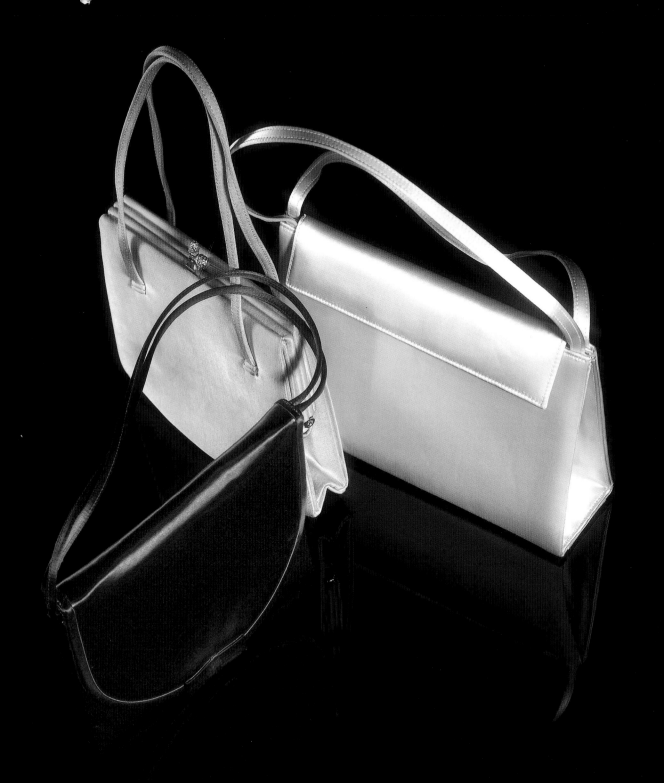

Plate 51 opposite Group of
Rayne evening bags.
Left: purple Duchesse satin
handbag with a flap and self-
covered bow. With matching
shoes (not illustrated).
British c.1975. T.220A–1976.
Middle: green-silk handbag
with acorn faux-diamond
clasp and double handle.
British, c.1970. Made by
Waldybag for Rayne.
T.218B–1976. Right: pink
Duchesse satin handbag
with a narrow flap and snap
fastening. With matching
shoes (not illustrated).
British, 1968. T.224A–1976.
Bags and shoes were often
dyed to match an outfit.
Rayne were a top-level
company, providing a
special dyeing service and
commissioning many
handbags from H. Wald & Co.

Plate 52 right Metal and faux
pearl *minaudière* bought at
Fior. British, 1956. By Evans.
Worn by Mrs Carol Howard at
her wedding on Boxing Day
1956. T.234:1-3–1998

patenting of a treatment to strengthen monogrammed canvas now used for handbags, and the Hermès 'Kelly' bag, named after Grace Kelly. Italy also started to play a leading role in the supply of quality goods, the most famous of which was Gucci with their bamboo-handled bag. The growth of the boutique in the 1950s allowed designers who had already turned their attention to accessories before the war to find an outlet and a growing audience for their more affordable ranges.

The three dominant styles of the 1950s were the classic, structured handbag on a metal frame of lacquered brass or steel, the clutch bag, and the open bucket bag, an elegant form of shopper. Handbags were used for their ability to complete an outfit, to tone with it: for example, a brown pigskin bag would be worn with tweeds; smart black patent with a 'little black dress' and high heels. Bags were also used to provide a dash of colour, an accent to an outfit, 'the tonic effect of a brilliant pink with black, alabaster with marigold' (*Vogue,* October 1955, p.118). Evening clutch bags were made in silver and gold

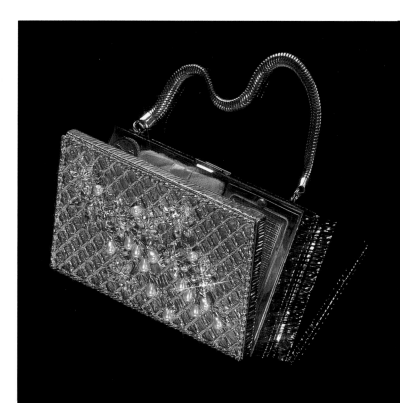

brocades, kid and diamanté, or in solid metal (plate 52), and outfits were composed as much as assembled. Leather bags in reversed calf, soft antelope, textured ostrich and hide for the country, with saddlestitching, were popular; there was a combination of materials, a softening of line in mohair and tweed with leather trimming, and, for summer, machine-made lace, linen, broderie anglaise, floral-print clutch bags from Liberty and printed silks by Zika Ascher.

Handbags became increasingly affordable for a wider range of society. Because of the invention of washable plastics, pastel colours were at last a possibility for everyone. In America, 'lucite', a new plastic that could be transparent or opaque, was used for moulding boxy handbags in a variety of ingenious and imaginative shapes, which were then ornately decorated and embellished. Plastic patent and calf, 'beadette' bags, glued on to a fabric base, and plastic coil bags were all available at low cost, while embossed plastic could replicate straw and linen textures, a fashion that came from Italy, perhaps reinforced by the trend for package holidays abroad. Genuine reptile skins returned, sometimes complete with head and claws. Expensive before the war and unaffordable during it, reptile skin had always been a status symbol, and a large black crocodile bag made by H. Wald & Co. cost £79 in 1952, a small fortune. By the late fifties, handbags were larger, and clutch bags exaggeratedly long as hemlines crept up (fig. 17); the December 1958 issue of *Vogue* noted that 'the bigger the better is the new philosophy for the handbag buyer'.

The 1960s

Of all the handbag styles of the 1950s to make the difficult transition into the age of informality and youth fashions, the narrow, long clutch at first succeeded, for it had always been thought suitable for a more youthful look, especially in pastel shades. Up until the early 1960s, handbags and shoes had possessed almost a moral quality in the pursuit of the fashionable ideal, while also being part of the codification of physical allure. All the old notions of correct dressing were broken down as youth fashion began to take hold, first started by the beatniks and students of the coffee-bar generation of the 1950s. The first bags to appeal to a generation of teenagers looking for a style that

Plate 53 opposite Tote bag made of paper printed in a floral pattern. British, c.1967. Disposable dresses, underwear and accessories became popular in the 1960s. T.35–1992

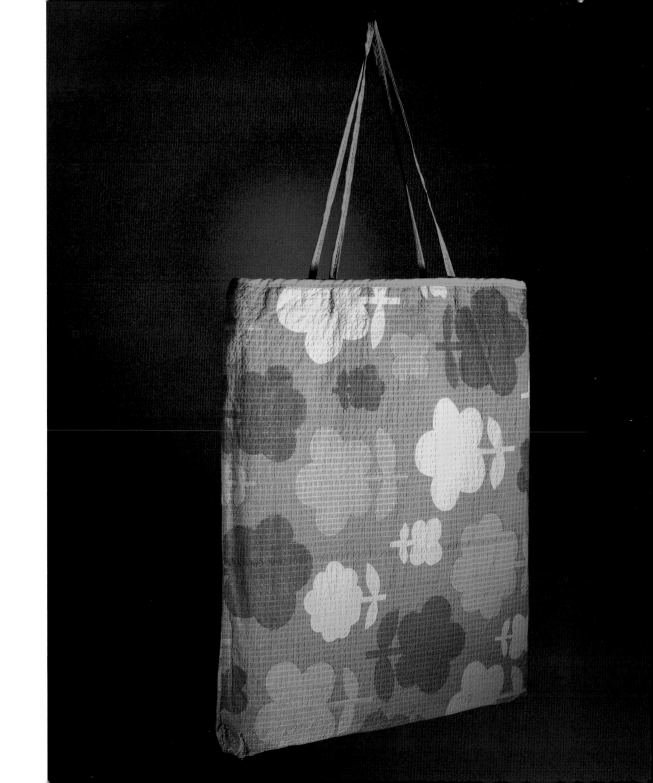

did not follow the generation before were versions of Chanel's shiny black-patent bag on a long gilt chain; PVC was bright and reflective, and fitted in with the angular, black-and-white look of Op Art, and many cheap versions were made. Although between 1961 and 1966 handbags hardly featured in fashion spreads, for they simply didn't look right, a consensus was gradually emerging. At risk of losing their entire business, handbag manufacturers were forced to respond to ever changing vogues, and the quantity of mass-produced, ready-to-wear and disposable fashion set a new tone.

Eventually the shoulder bag dominated, at first small and dainty, it swung on long chains or thin straps, in keeping with the animation of fashion and the informal, childlike qualities of the miniskirt. Fashion photography of the time reflected these 'Swinging' fashions in stark contrast to the posed 1950s models. Mary Quant, who opened her first boutique in 1965, said in her autobiography (1966): 'I want to invent … new fashion accessories that are up to date with the changing ways of life.' Modernity was celebrated, influenced by Courrèges' space-age collection of 1964 and fine-art movements such as Op Art and Pop Art. Plastic dresses, vinyl, PVC, chain-mail minis, disposable printed paper dresses and matching bags (plate 53) were all the rage, complemented by white beaded purses or flat bags with cutouts for handles. The V&A has a flat silver-leather bag with straight perspex handles by actress-turned-handbag designer Sally Jess. The new trouser suit was worn with both multi-pocketed shoulder bags and large shoppers. Psychedelic patterns and, later, flower power introduced a romantic and then ethnic look to fashion.

By the late 1960s, larger satchels and fabric shoulder bags began to predominate, brought back by the first young travellers to India. Afghan coats and bags, carpet bags, patchwork and embroidery and ex-army shoulder bags dovetailed with the emergence of an interest in hand-crafted as opposed to machine-made goods, supported by a huge influx of imported, ethnic items. Different boundaries and experiences merged into a look that had developed in less than a decade, one that was individualistic, expressive, even, by the early 1970s, subversive.

The 1970s

It's all in the bag ... combinations of fur and reversed calf; leather and webbing; a patchwork of lizard in scarlet, orange, Irish green, taupe; camera cases; cartridge cases; mail pouches ... Bags strapped right under the arm; long-strap bags slapping the thigh; Moroccan studding and embroidery; harness brass on fake python, sleek as Rotten Row. (US *Vogue*, November 1970, p.89)

The decade started with cropped cardigans, Oxford bags and neat clutch bags, and, alternatively, tapestry shoes and large carpet bags. Adrienne Mann made suede 'squaw' bags with beading and long fringing, and Thea Porter, in the November issue of British *Vogue* 1970, p.116, showed 'crushed icing velvet' trousers, tucked into long boots and bags of 'kaleidoscopic embroidery'. A growing informality in dress and a tendency towards layering and mixing different weights and fabrics allowed the handbag, once so formal, to relax into a functional receptacle that was to be used for all occasions, to become battered and familiar.

Patchwork leather bags, brass-studded suede and all sorts prevailed. Colour was celebrated with striped knitwear, teamed up with Lesley Slight's appliqué bags and paint-box gloves from the London boutique Bus Stop, each finger a different colour. A growing interest in craft was supported by top designer Jean Muir, who showed leather-appliqué clutch and shoulder bags designed by Nigel Lofthouse. Couture houses such as Saint Laurent Rive Gauche were represented by monogrammed beige-canvas and brown-leather shoulder bags, while Gucci had leather and topstitched shoulder bags with dog-leash fittings.

Soon, large, soft envelope bags began to dominate, and in 1974 a new style was seen, typified by a novel-thick clutch in smart ginger-and-cream stripes by Christopher Trill. Bright primary colours (plate 54) began to be accompanied by a new palette of pastels. Long floral dresses were accessorised with 1930s' jewellery and matched with floral bags such as Clive Shilton's pastel quilted clutches, which confirmed a nostalgic feel as a new prettiness crept into fashion. By the middle of the decade, this floral interest had turned to Chinese silk

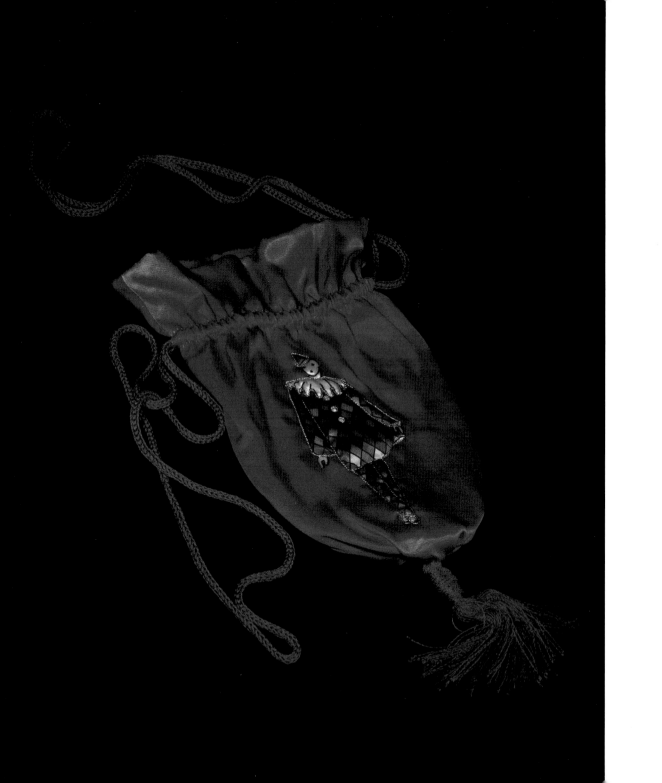

Plate 54 opposite Red satin drawstring bag with clown appliqué. Scottish, 1979. By Chris Clyne. Part of a 'Harlequin' outfit. T.224F–1980

Fig. 18 right 'Musette' bag of string net with metal coils and brown-leather strap; quilted cotton gabardine and pigskin shooting bag. British, 1976. By Mulberry. Part of a unisex ensemble in natural materials and colours accessorised with multiple bags and belts slung around the body. A billiard-pocket makers supplied the string component of the bag. T.32:5–1997; T.32.8–1997

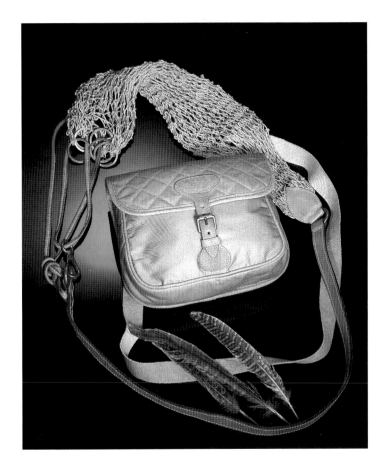

embroideries, reflected by tiny embroidered shoulder purses on long fine straps by Jap, followed by numerous inexpensive versions in import shops.

Shoulder bags returned, increasingly large and squashy in leather or canvas, in textured leathers and buttery suedes, moving away from the ethnic look. Two leading companies were Loewe and the Italian company Enny, who claimed that theirs were 'Bags for Today's Women'. These were becoming larger, fuller and heavier – and, as *Vogue* said of their contents, in its November 1976 issue, 'the only thing more revealing is a medicine cupboard'. Carried slung across the shoulders, with their numerous pockets and zips, most women seemed equipped for anything in the new age of feminism. Handbags for British traditional country pursuits had long been made by companies such as Burberry and Simpson, and a newcomer in the 1970s, Mulberry, introduced hunting and fishing bags characterised by embossed leather (fig. 18).

Evening wear took on a relaxed sophistication, with diminutive versions of the clutch on long shoulder chains. A black-suede envelope bag on a strap of twisted black satin and diamanté from Charles Jourdan of 1977 was worn with black silk shirt and pants and gold-kid cummerbund.

Good health, shiny hair, outdoor pursuits and a positive attitude belied the underlying nostalgia of the 1970s. Bags that had started out as handcrafted and individualistic were discarded in favour of those that were defiantly expensive, clearly identifiable goods, consumer icons, despite Gucci's claim in an advertisement of 1968: 'We realise that Gucci cannot dictate a personal style … you will be able to choose the style that suits your personal taste.' Unlike the investment handbag of the fifties that worked hard for its living, these handbags inspired obsessive desire and, of course, a million copies. Fashion became a serious pursuit for the professional woman. Not mentioned in the top magazines of the late 1970s was the emergence of punk and the growth of street-power style. Anti-establishment fashions had much to pit themselves against in the Thatcherite '80s.

The 1980s

When Your Own Initials are Enough. (Bottega Veneta's advertising campaign, 1984)

Handbags in the 1980s managed to combine two seemingly disparate elements in British dress: a sympathy for the country with an instinct for survival in a highly industrialised city life. Mulberry epitomised the fashion for protective bags and clothes inspired by traditional country wear, despite the fact that they were more often seen in an urban environment. With a concern for health and fitness, sports bags and shoes were a second group of accessories that influenced high fashion. Work-bags, on the other hand, took on a fevered search for

Plate 55 opposite
Rhinestone encrusted 'Fabergé Egg' evening bag with trademark mirror and tasseled comb. USA, 1983. By Judith Leiber. Judith Leiber is best known for her jewelled *minaudières* and idiosyncratic metal vanity cases. Each is jewelled by hand, and they are collector's items. T.511:1-4–1997

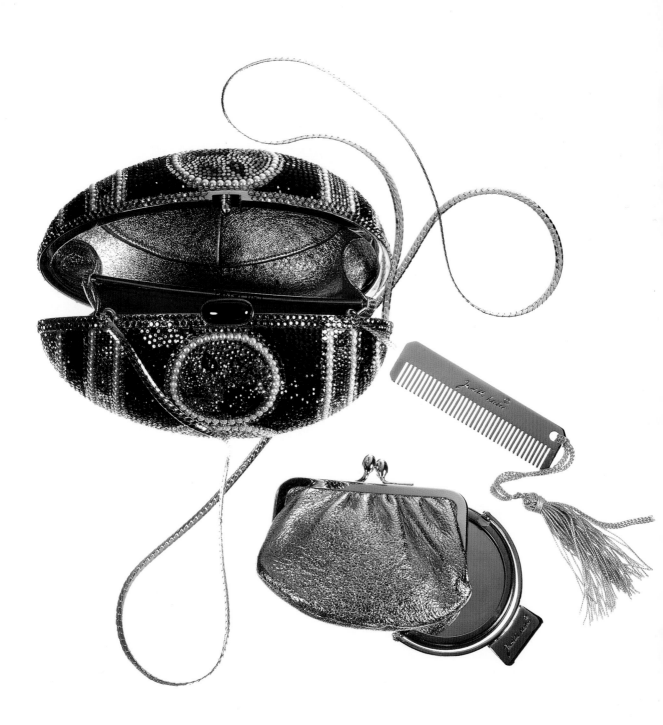

order and control, with ever increasing miniaturisation, as technology got to grips with the calculator and the filofax. Advice that would once have been given on being stylishly accessorised and colour co-ordinated was now devoted to organisation. In 1988 Donna Karan explained her solution to the enormously heavy tote: 'systems', 'a small evening bag that slips into a tote, a leather knapsack that distributes weight between the shoulders and holds, for outside lunches, a small shoulder bag' (US *Vogue,* September 1988, p.233).

Bags began to be advertised not only as vital accessories to complete a look but also with a confidence that demanded that they be seen in their own right. Some were luxury items, clearly destined to be collectibles rather than fashion statements (plate 55). Others, changing with each season, created a great sense of competitiveness and were copied by a wider range of consumers. The good handbag, always expensive, always an investment, became associated with conspicuous consumption for their designer was always conspicuously indicated, and waiting lists increased.

In some cases this snobbery was inverted, as in Bottega Veneta's advertising campaign of 1984: 'When Your Own Initials are Enough'. Karl Lagerfeld, taking over as chief designer at Chanel, began reworking the 2.55 in ever more ingenious ways and shapes, in washable jersey, denim, rubber and terry cloth. In the same year the company's advertising campaign subverted the norm by showing a fashionably dressed model photographing three self-conscious and unfashionable girls awkwardly holding gilt-chained Chanel bags, playing with the idea of the quilting and the double-C as signifiers in whatever context they were seen. Hermès, in contrast, relied on tradition, with an allusion in their advertisements to the company's saddlery past and a reference to their products as 'savage elegance'.

Knapsacks had been in the air for some time; Jean-Charles de Castelbajac made a backpack jacket in 1984 with room for shopping. But, in 1985, Miuccia Prada introduced the black nylon knapsack that inspired a wave of designer versions from Vuitton and Chanel to Fendi and Gucci, before filtering down to become the first totally unisex bag, which remains ubiquitous.

Plate 56 opposite Bag of ivory and chocolate-brown leather. Italian, 1996. By Moschino. The Moschino label was launched in 1983, their trademark being a good-natured mockery of *haute couture* that became highly fashionable in itself. In this case the handbag is adorned surrealistically with 'melted' chocolate. The advertising campaign for this bag was set in a baker's shop. T.582:-1996

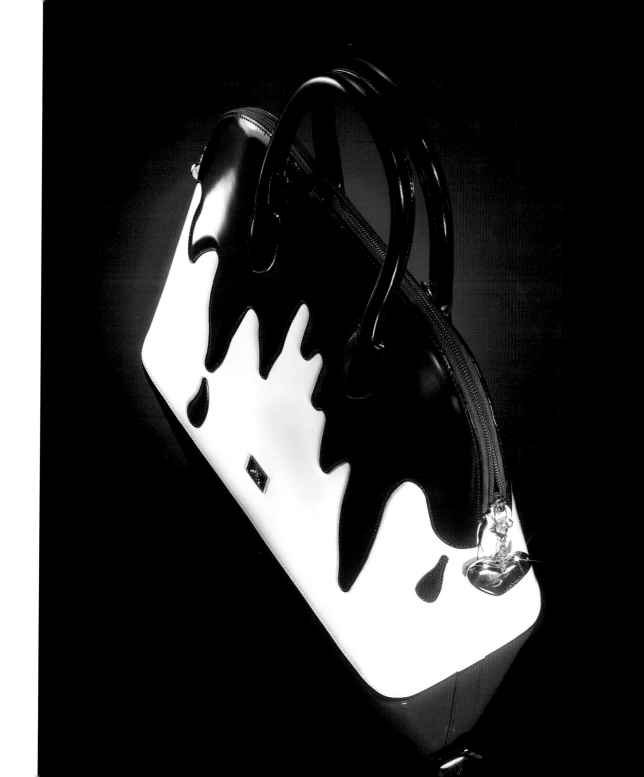

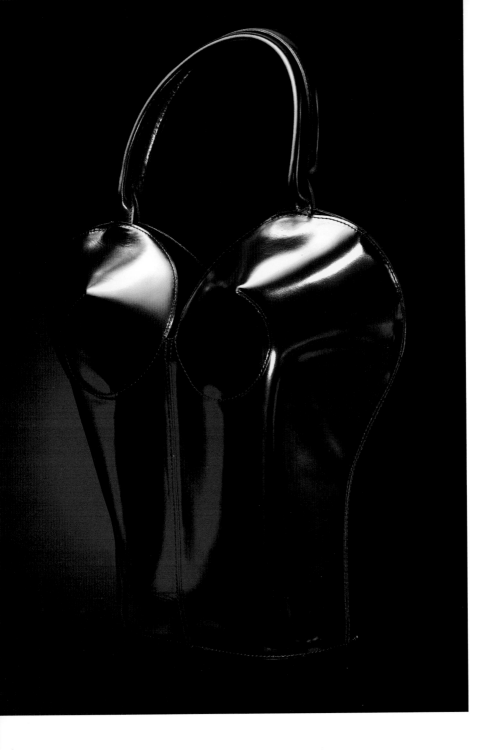

Plate 57 left Black leather bust-shaped handbag. Japanese, 1990s. By Issey Miyake. This bag plays on the idea of the femininity of the handbag – formed into a hollow torso it is subtle and disconcerting. T.149–1991

Plate 58 opposite Silver-coloured angel wings back-pack by Kitty Percy. British, *c.* 1994. Acquired for the Street Style Exhibition at the V&A in 1996, the rucksack is transformed into angelic silver wings. T.605–1994

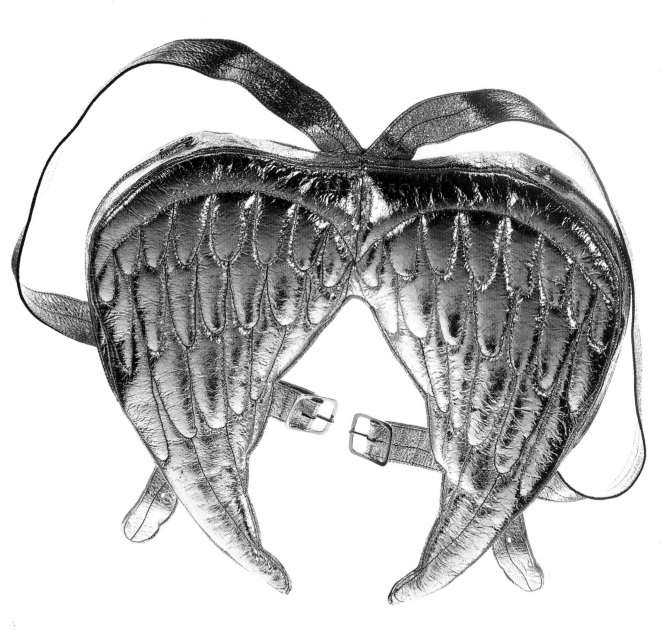

The 1990s

In the early 1990s, small designer bags with giant Hs and CCs swung all over London, New York and Paris, and only the trained eye could distinguish the real article from the fake. Stalwarts such as Jane Shilton continued to provide quality for many women with their affordable and well-made wide range of bags. Shoe shops and boutique groups such as Hobbs, Next and Warehouse produced accessories that perfectly complemented their styles. Handbag manufacture, mainly in the East, turned out a cut-price production line of leather bags. Meanwhile, fashion designers featured more and more accessories at their catwalk shows, with hats, bags and shoes supplying the fizz, and the sales, for many collections (plates 56 and 57).

Rucksacks continued to be popular and youthful. Comfortable and practical, they typified the early 1990s modern, minimalist approach to fashion with casual accessories and an egalitarian feel. Men, women, students, tourists and ultra-fashionable clubbers could all find something to suit (plate 58). Smart handbags remained small and shapely, with twisted-gilt bracelet handles from Saint Laurent, quilted denim from Chanel and the Hermès signature Kelly bag, miniaturised and worn around the neck like a trophy. Diversification was a key word, and just as the top designers had quickly followed the launch of a collection with accessories, so the great accessory houses such as Hermès turned their hand to making clothes.

A further group of British accessory makers emerged in the 1990s, in the long tradition of the artist–craftsmen. These include Bill Amberg (fig. 19), a leather-goods designer and maker who runs a small company in London creating the finest handbags and briefcases, amongst many other things; Nathalie Hambro who works in metal mesh and felt (fig. 20) and Emily Jo Gibbs who creates delicate purses and bags in metals and silks (plate 59). Anya Hindmarch (see bags on back of this book's jacket) and Lulu Guinness (plate 60) have both contributed greatly to the revival of the small, feminine handbag, while in 1997, the milliner Philip Treacy designed the first of his small collections of beautifully sculptured handbags (see plate 1).

The importance of accessories in this decade is indicated by the number of top designers producing collections, from Paul Smith to

Fig. 19 top right 'Small Rocket' bag of black bridle leather, cast-aluminium handles, nickel clamped feet and green-suede lining. British, 1996. By Bill Amberg. This is a classic briefcase with a contemporary feel, by one of Britain's most talented leather workers.
T.629–1996

Fig. 20 below right Stainless-steel mesh handbag with metal buttons and leather cord. British, 1997. By Nathalie Hambro. Launched in 1997, Nathalie Hambro's fashion accessories are hand-crafted and produced in small numbered limited editions.
T.672–1997

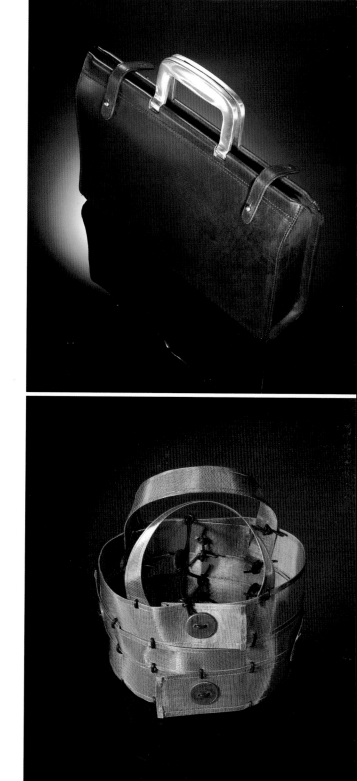

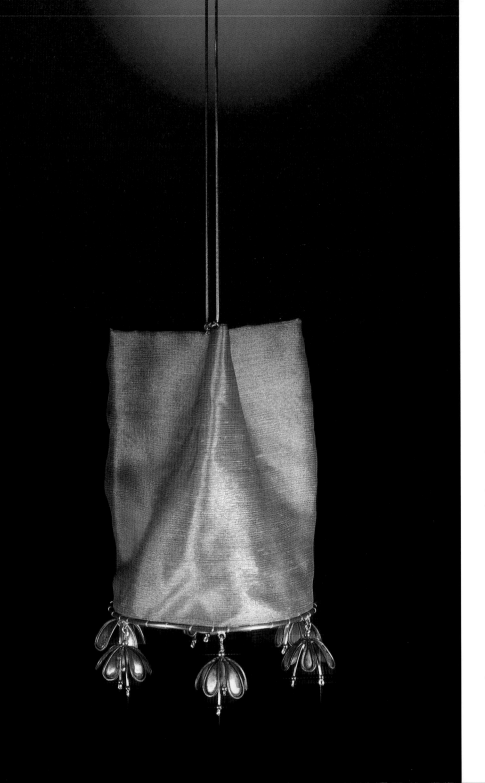

Plate 59 left Silk drawstring purse with circular base, supported by a silver ring from which fuschia-shaped metal tassels hang. British, 1998. By Emily Jo Gibbs. With fine silver chain handle. T.416–1998

Plate 60 opposite 'House' handbag in black satin with a red-suede 'roof'. British, 1998. By Lulu Guinness. Hand-embroidered in England. Lulu Guinness's designs have been highly influential in the revival of feminine, glamorous bags for both day and evening. The designer has recently joined a group of other young accessory makers to produce a diffusion range for Debenham's. T.418:1&2–1998

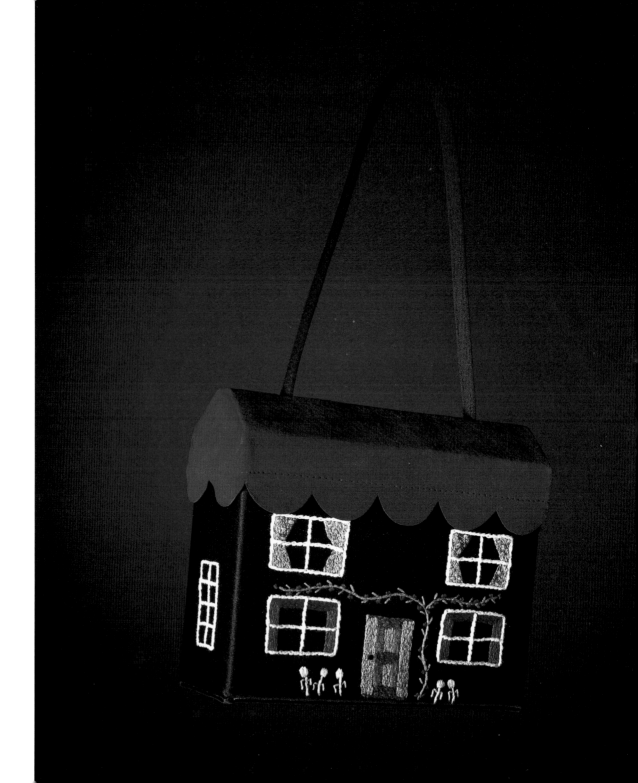

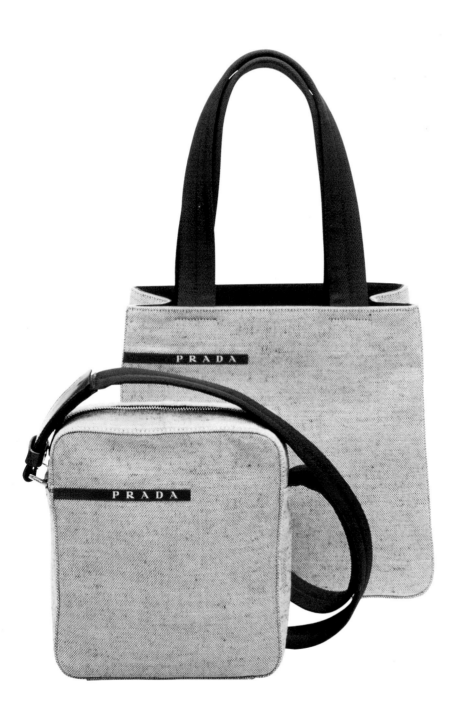

Plate 61 left Two red leather bags. British, 1998. By Prada. Photograph courtesy of Prada

Jil Sander. Long-established leatherwork companies have seen an upsurge in their success, from Goldpfeil through Tanner Krolle to Ferragamo. Luxury evening bags are produced by Paloma Picasso, Nina Ricci, Lacroix, Daniel Swarovski, Hervé Léger, Armani and Erickson Beamon. Such bags add instant glamour to any ensemble. Handbags are now made in a bewildering choice of styles and materials – yet trends such as Fendi's baguette bag, Miu Miu's waist bag, beaded one-offs, little Eastern bags and Prada's flat waist and leg bags of 1999 demonstrate the diversity of styles and prices today.

In 1998, Chanel released Karl Lagerfeld's '2005' handbag (plates 62 and 63), the descendant of the 2.55 created by Gabrielle Chanel in 1955 and still influential half a century on. Utilising the latest in technology, its rigid, lightweight polyethylene shell is clothed by hand over an aluminium frame in tight black jersey, tweed or leather. Formed to sit comfortably against the hips, its shape also recalls the female body, while its interior is a fetishistic dream, with corset-style laced mobile-phone holder, zips and pockets. Destined to become the next cult handbag, it epitomises the extraordinary potency of this small accessory.

Both private and personal, handbags also provide the finishing touch to any fashionable ensemble. Their design is inspired by a heady mix of function and fashion, giving them a unique role as expressive companions to women's lives. In her book *Fighting Fashion*, Helen Storey succinctly pays tribute to this (1996, p.163):

Today's young designers must consider where their edge lies and, if it is remotely blurred, should consider sharpening it. For me, this much needed quality has already partially emerged, but for now it is located in the small. It dresses the furthest north, south, east and west of woman – her edges, her finishing touches ... The loudest noise in our industry's recent history has been the whisper and tight snap of a handbag clasp. A bag by Prada has signified that the power of dressing women in the nineties lies not in a total look for her every waking moment but in the 'special' about her.

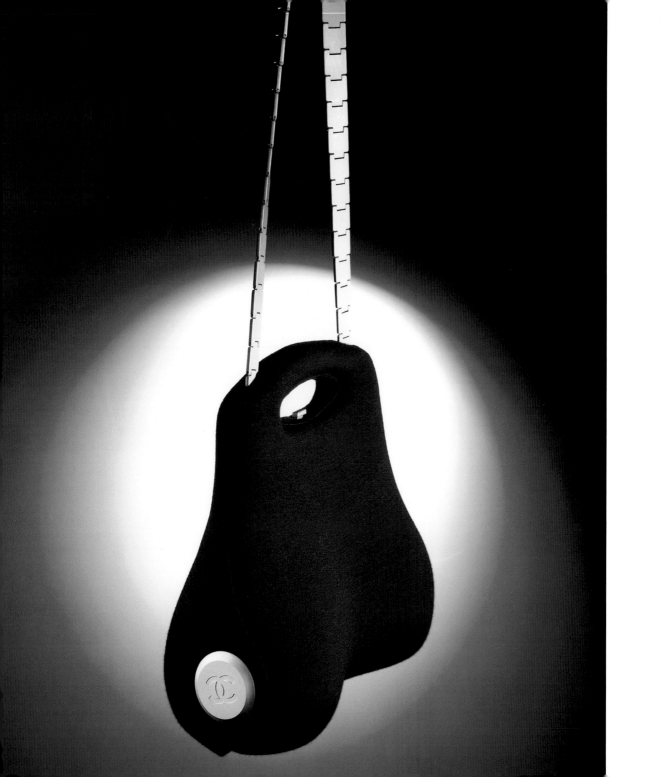

Plates 62 opposite and 63 right '2005' handbag, black jersey covered polyethylene shell with 'bodyfriendly' curves, snap-lock fastener and optional aluminium ribbon strap with nylon interior pockets, including laced mobile-phone holder. French, 1998. By Chanel, designed by Karl Lagerfeld. The new cult handbag of the late 1990s. T.7–1999

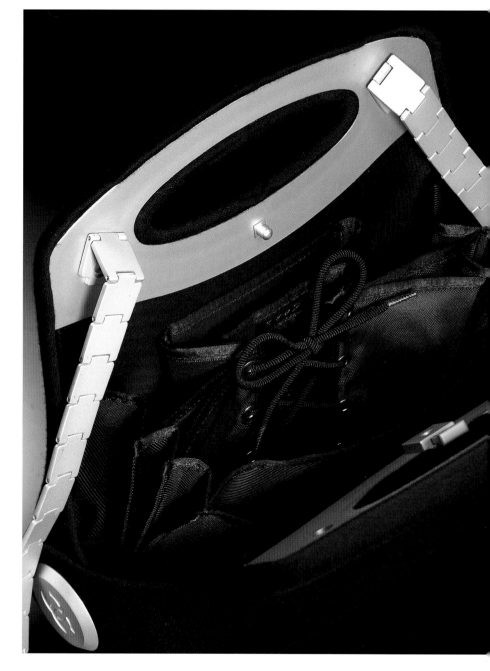

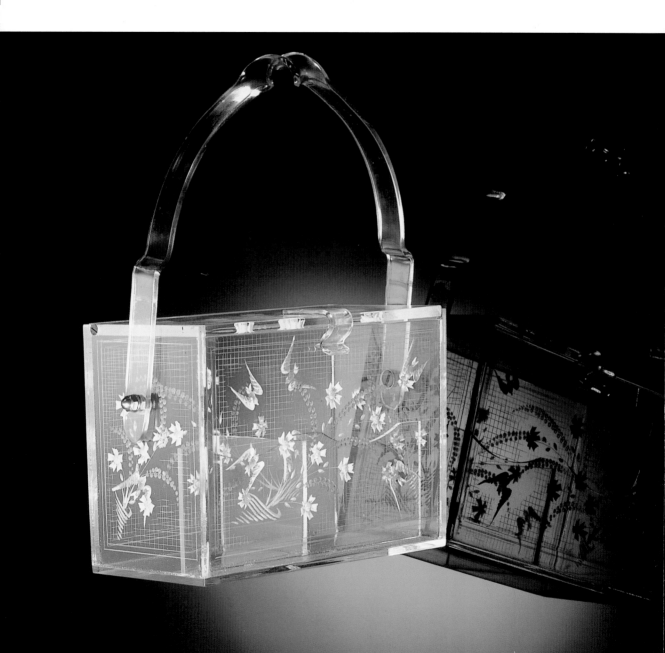

Major UK Dress Collections Featuring Bags

Brighton Museum & Art Gallery
Church Street
Brighton
East Sussex
BN1 1UE

Central Museum and Art Gallery
Guildhall Road
Northampton
NN1 1DP

Gallery of English Costume
Platt Hall
Rusholme
Manchester
M14 5LL

Lotherton Hall
Aberford
Leeds
LS25 3EB

Museum of Costume
Assembly Rooms
Bennett Street
Bath
Avon
BA1 2QH

Museum of Costume & Textiles
51 Castle Gate
Nottingham
NG1 6AF

Museum of London
London Wall
London
EC2Y 5HN

Museum of Welsh Life
St Fagans
Cardiff
CF5 6XB

National Museum of Scotland
Chambers Street
Edinburgh
EH1 1JF

Shambellie House Museum of
Costume
New Abbey
Nr Dumfries
DG2 8HQ

Snowshill Manor
Snowshill
nr Broadway
Worcester
WR12 7JU

Victoria & Albert Museum
South Kensington
London
SW7 2RL

Worthing Museum & Art Gallery
Chapel Road
Worthing
West Sussex
BN11 1HP

York Castle Museum
York
YO1 1RY

Plate 64 opposite Clear
perspex handbag with
engraved bird and floral
decoration. Possibly French,
early 1950s. T.632:–1–1996

Selected Bibliography

Arnold, Janet *Queen Elizabeth's Wardrobe Unlock'd* (Leeds, Maney, 1988)

Austen, Jane (ed) Chapman, R.W. *Letters* (Oxford Edition)

Blum, Stella (ed) *Ackermann's Costume Plates, Women's Fashions in England, 1818-1828* (New York, Dover, 1978)

Blum, Stella *Designs by Erté: fashion drawings and illustrations from Harper's Bazaar* (New York, Dover, 1976)

Boucher, Francois *A History of Costume in the West* (London, Thames and Hudson, 1987)

Bradfield, Nancy *Costume in Detail 1730–1930* (London, Harrap, 1968)

Bridgeman, Harriet and Drury, Elizabeth (eds) *Needlework, an illustrated history* (London, Paddington Press Ltd, 1978)

Buck, Ann *Dress in Eighteenth Century England* (London, Batsford, 1980)

Byrde, Penelope *A Frivolous Distinction, Fashion and Needlework in the Works of Jane Austen* (Bath City Council, 1979)

Clabburn, Pamela *The Needleworker's Dictionary* (London, Morrant, 1978)

Coke, Lady Mary *Lady Mary Coke, Letters and Journals* 1756-1774 (Kingsmere reprints, Bath 1970)

Cunnington, C.W. *English Women's Clothing in the 19th century* (London, Faber & Faber, 1937)

Cunnington,C.W. *English Women's Clothing in the Present century*, (London, Faber & Faber, 1952)

Cunnington, C.W. and P. *Handbook of English Medieval Costume* (London, Faber & Faber, 1952)

Cunnington, C.W. and P. *Handbook of English Costume in the 16th Century* (London, Faber & Faber, reprinted 1970)

Cunnington, C.W. and P. *Handbook of English Costume in the 17th Century* (London, Faber & Faber, reprinted 1972)

Cunnington, C.W. and P. *Handbook of English Costume in the 18th Century* (London, Faber & Faber, reprinted 1972)

Cunnington, C.W. and P. *Handbook of English Costume in the 19th Century* (London, Faber & Faber, reprinted 1970)

Cunnington, C.W. and P. and Charles Beard *A Dictionary of English Costume* (A&C Black, 1960)

Dooner, Kate *Plastic Handbags* (Pennsylvania, Schiffer Publishing Ltd, 1992)

Double, W.C. *Design and Construction of Handbags* (Oxford, OUP, 1960)

Egan, Geoff and Pritchard, Frances *Dress Accessories c1150–c1450, Medieval Finds from Excavations in London* (HMSO for the Museum of London, 1991)

Ettinger, Roseann *Handbags* (Pennsylvania, Schiffer Publishing Ltd, 1991)

Foster, Vanda *Bags & Purses* (London, Batsford, 1982)

Ginsburg, Madeleine *Victorian Dress in Photographs* (London, Batsford, reprinted 1988)

Groves, Sylvia *The History of Needlework Tools and Accessories* (London, Country Life Ltd, 1966)

Keppel, Sonia *Edwardian Daughter* (Delafield, 1958)

Leiber, Judith *The Artful Handbag* (Harry N. Abrams, 1995)

Llanover, Lady (ed) *The Autobiography and Correspondence of Mary Granville, Mrs Delany* (1861–1)

Lurie, Alison *The Language of Clothes* (Hamlyn, 1982)

Mazza, Samuele *In the Bag* (San Francisco, Chronicle Books, 1997)

Piponnier, Francoise and Mane, Perrine *Dress in the Middle Ages* (New Haven and London, Yale University Press, 1997)

Ribeiro, Aileen *Dress in 18th Century Europe 1715–1789* (New York, Holmes & Meier, 1985)

Ribeiro, Aileen *Fashion in the French Revolution* (London, Batsford, 1998)

Ribeiro, Aileen *Dress and Morality* (New York, Holmes & Meier, 1986)

Rothstein, Nathalie (ed) *Barbara Johnson's Album of Fashions and Fabrics* (London, Thames & Hudson, 1987)

Rutt, Richard *A History of Hand Knitting*, Bishop of Leicester (London, Batsford, 1987)

Tomalin, Claire *Jane Austen, A Life* (London, Penguin ,1998)

Wilcox, Claire *A Century of Style: Bags* (United Kingdom, Apple, 1998)

Wingfield Digby, George *Elizabethan Embroidery* (London, Faber & Faber, 1963)

Index